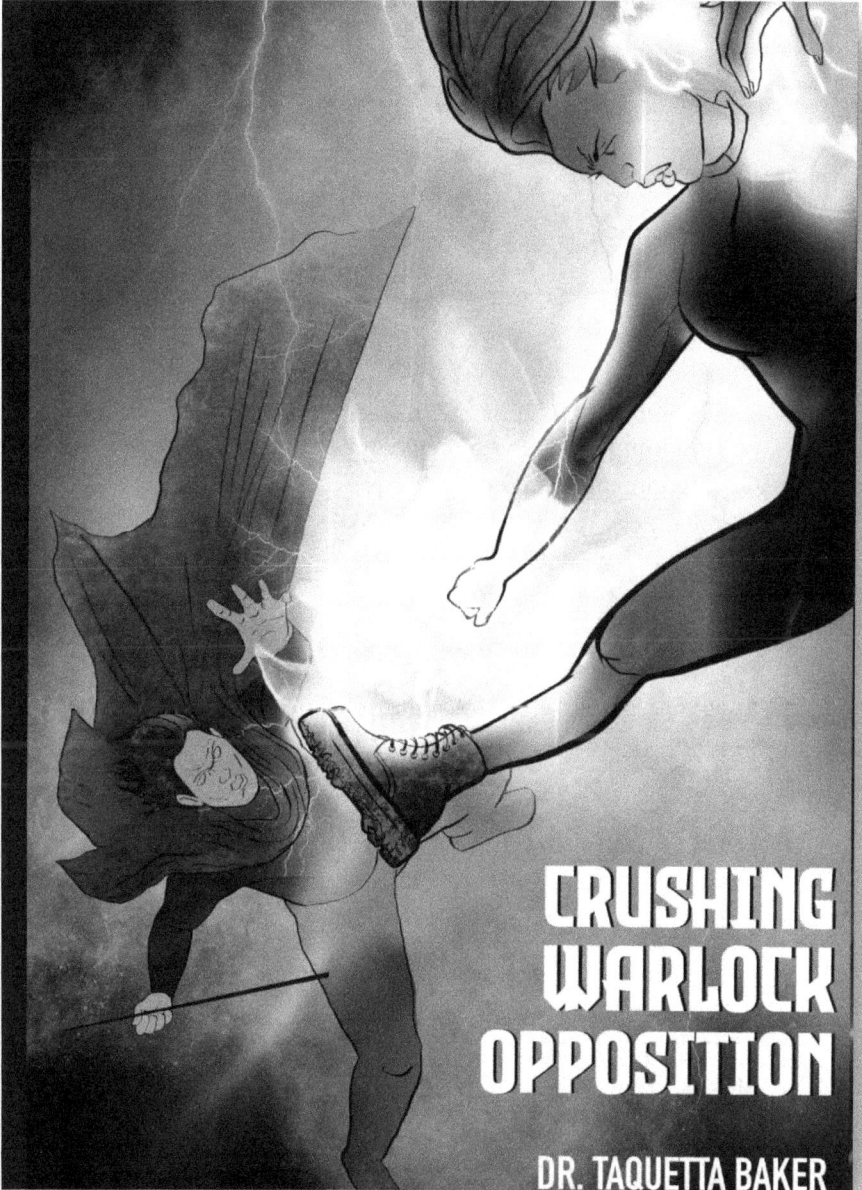

CRUSHING
WARLOCK
OPPOSITION

DR. TAQUETTA BAKER

Kingdom Shifters Christian Empowerment Center

Teaching People to Sustain in Spiritual Wellness

CRUSHING THE WARLOCK SPIRIT

---

kingdomshifterscec@gmail.com
kingdomwellnesscenter@gmail.com
kingdomshifters.com
kswu.net

Connect with Taquetta via Facebook or YouTube

Dr. TAQUETTA BAKER

Kingdom Shifters Publications
Muncie, IN

Book Synopsis

God has been speaking to me about how the warlock spirit will increase his operation as women arise to take their place of leadership and entrepreneurship in the earth. The warlock spirit will come to steal, kill, and destroy the virtue, seed, and vision of the women. It will seek to knock chosen women off their throne of destiny.

Because these women have been faithful, sanctified, self-sacrificing, and sold out to God, God is rewarding them for their diligence, destiny preparation, and wellness. Satan, on the other hand, wants to present these chosen women as usurpers of authority who are ill-equipped to reign in the earth. He wants to mislabel them as Jezebels, Delilahs, Athaliahs, and witches, who do not regard the role of men. However, these women are God's chosen - His Esthers, Deborahs, Marys, Marthas, Jehoshebas, Ruths, Hannahs, Elizabeths, and Sarahs. Many of them have the anointing of Joseph, Moses, Elijsha, David, and Paul upon their lives and they are significant to the next SHIFTING dispensation in the earth.

God wants his chosen women to be equipped for the purpose of discerning the warlock spirit and understanding how it operates to charm, corrupt, and murder them. He wants the sounding of His alarm regarding this hooking spirit. He also wants the younger women to be taught how to avoid the trappings of the warlock spirit so they can sustain in destiny and in the vision, He has granted to their hands. To God's chosen women: Arise! Take your place and do not lend your virtue to warlocks!!

ENDORSEMENT

Dr. Taquetta Baker has masterfully written on a very hidden topic that has wreaked havoc on many in the Body of Christ. With her vast experience in spiritual warfare and ministering deliverance, combined with her incredible study and knowledge of the Word of God, *Crushing Warlock Opposition* is powerfully informative and an excellent weapon of war.

Not only does Dr. Taquetta dive deep into the nature, characteristics, and tactics of a warlock but also includes powerful keys of freedom, prompts and deliverance activations.

I highly endorse *Crushing Warlock Opposition* to every individual believer, church, small group leader, apostolic hub, or leadership team as an essential tool in your spiritual warfare arsenal! You will be well equipped to not only identify warlocks but how to *not* to be deceived or seduced by this veiled and cunning opposition; crushing it completely. Get ready for FREEDOM!

Jennifer Nestler
Founder, Esther Company
www.Esther-Company.com

TABLE OF CONTENTS

VISION STATEMENT

Kingdom Shifters Ministries (KSM) is a Jesus-focused ministry with a heart to see people, churches and communities healed, delivered, and liberated to walk in the fullness of their destiny. The ministry is founded upon *Ephesians 4:10-13*, where Jesus gave the five-fold ministry (some apostles, some prophets, some evangelists, some pastors, some teachers) as a gift to the church for the perfecting and edification of the saints, equipping for the saving of souls, and to further establish the kingdom and the glory of heaven in the earth. KSM operates under this mandate while using various ministry styles, business organizations, and marketplace outlets in order to shift people and atmospheres out of darkness and into God's light, so they can journey in and through the ordained purposes God has placed inside of them.

Taquetta Baker, Founder

Taquetta was adopted by her aunt at two weeks old. She was raised with four brothers in East St. Louis and has been a fighter since she was a little girl. God has transformed that fighting personality into a spiritual warrior in his kingdom! She has a testimony of having her fists turned into hands of prayer, complete with the gift of healing and faith for miracles, signs, and wonders to manifest.

God transformed Taquetta from one who frequented nightclubs and battled alcoholism to one with a strategy to empower others in destiny. Her name means "child of love," and she carries that mantle of unconditionally loving and restoring the unlovable.

Taquetta is gifted at empowering and assisting people with launching ministries, businesses, and books. She provides mentoring, counseling, coaching, and destiny development through her Kingdom Wellness Counseling and Mentoring Center. She has written her very own Kingdom Wellness Counseling Theory and will be launching a certified program to train mental health leaders and deliverers. The program includes training on how to operate in healings and how to SHIFT people into sustainable wellness.

Taquetta flows through the wells of deliverance, revival reform, warfare, and worship. She carries the mantle, not only of her spiritual mother, Dr. Kathy Williams, but also of her overseer and apostolic mother, Dr. Jackie Green. Her mantle includes an apostolic mandate of judging and establishing God's kingdom in people, ministries, communities, and regions. Taquetta has over 22 years of deliverance and warfare experience. She is skilled in dismantling principalities and strongholds in people, generations, and regions, and is keen in seeking God for strategic insight on how to overthrow the powers and systems of darkness.

Taquetta travels throughout the United States and in foreign missions. She has mentored and established altar workers, and dance, deliverance, and prophetic ministries. Taquetta ministers in the fine arts, five-fold ministry, deliverance, healings, miracles, atmospheric worship, apostolic reform, and all manners of prayer. She empowers and trains people in their destiny and life visions. She walks the walk and rejoices at the expansion of God's kingdom!

Taquetta's Credentials

- Founder of Kingdom Shifters Ministries (KSM), Indiana
- Founder of Kingdom Wellness Counseling and Mentoring Center
- Author of over 38 books and 2 prayer decree CD's
- Doctorate in Ministry from Rapha Deliverance University
- Master's Degree in Community Counseling with an emphasis on Marriage, Children and Family Counseling
- Bachelor's Degree in Psychology
- Associates Degree in Business Administration
- Certified Life Coach, Certified Professional Coach, Certified Executive Leadership Coach through the Breakthrough Coaching and Leadership Academy
- Therapon Belief Therapist Certification from the Therapon Institute (faith-based counseling)
- Board of Directors for New Day Community Ministries, Inc.
- Graduate of Eagles Dance Institute under Dr. Pamela Hardy; Licensed in the area of liturgical dance
- Apostolic Ordination by Bishop Jackie Green, Founder of JGM-National Prayer Life Institute (Phoenix, AZ)
- Previous ministry service as prophet, visionary for Shekinah Expressions Dance Troupe, teacher, member of presbytery, overseer for altar workers' ministry

SHIFT FORTH NOW!

Warlock Prophetic Warning

Word Released July 19, 2021

As women arise to be used for the glory of God, the spirit of feminism and the spirit of the warlock is being increasingly unleashed as a counterassault to take women down from their throne of destiny. The feminist spirit causes women to believe that they do not need men. It also attempts to strip men of their roles and positions in the earth. The feminist spirit's agenda is accomplished, mainly outside of the body of Christ, by witches posing as justice advocates for women. These witches cause people to believe that their agenda is *"for the good of all mankind."* However, the attack of the warlock spirit will increasingly infiltrate the body of Christ, especially as mixture and effeminacy becomes the norm. Women who have held sacred values and kept themselves consecrated before God, will be subject to warlocking men and strong macho-type women who will come disguised as God's man or woman of valor. They will come with sly moves, crafty words, seducing tongues, seeking to steal the sacred virtues of God's chosen queens.

The enemy is angry at the bruising of the head of his kingdom, especially in the area of entrepreneurialism. And he's angry at the fact that women are making the sacrifice to live in purity and in alignment with God. There is also a rage against the generational work that women have done in prayer and in their stance as curse breakers in their family lines. Women's unwillingness to compromise their standards and their being content in their lives whether they have a man or not has broken the generational cycles of warlocks who have able to operate from generation to generation. Not that the women do not desire a man, but they have been unwilling to compromise.

The unleashing of the warlock spirit is the enemy's attempt to regain ground that God's women have taken in these terrains. It is also for the purpose of embarrassing the women whom God has chosen to arise in this hour, causing it appear as if women have usurped men and are being judged, rather than succeeding in the truth that God is merely rewarding these women for their faithfulness. This is indeed the hour for women to rise up and be used in the fullness of their destinies and callings. It is the hour for women to advance the Kingdom of God, to align with men, and even become empowered by men to SHIFT forth in all that God is desiring them to do in the earth.

It is essential to train and equip women to identify, expose, judge, and eject the spirit of the warlock. Women also need to be aware of where they are when dealing with hope deferred in waiting for their purposed mates. If they opt to date and explore options, they must have clarity in understanding what they can handle in consideration of God's standard for what they need in a mate. Women simply must be weaponized in clarity, truth and safeguards against the warlock. For it will be the craftiness, charm, and deceit of the warlock that will hook and lock the women of God in a war for their virtue and destiny.

We must realize that this assault has already gripped the earth as women, girls, and children are being trafficked by the predatory warlock. This terrorist spirit has no regard for the lives of the female. He just wants to sell her power, virtue, and seed for personal gain.

"Train my young women against this spirit. My hand is on the younger generation. The young women are being drawn away right at the crossroads of destiny. They are mistaking lust for love. They are mistaking the voice of the serpent - the knowledge of the serpent for my voice. Knowledge is puffed up. It is vain. It is the root of deceit. They are being charmed off my course by slithering tongues and seducing ways. Give them truth and equip them for the terrorist serpent warlock so My hand can cause them to reign in destiny with me.

I am sending this warning not to fear men but that they become equipped against the enemy. Become equipped in discerning so that you can stand as a crown of diadem for My glory."

2Corinthians 11:3 But I fear, lest by any means, as the serpent beguiled Eve through his subtilty, so your minds should be corrupted from the simplicity that is in Christ.

Beguiled means to deceive and to seduce wholly.

Subtility is *panurgic* in Greek and means:
1. adroitness (subtle ease and ingenuity)
2. i.e. (in a bad sense) trickery or sophistry: cunning, craftiness, subtilty
3. craftiness, cunning, a specious or false wisdom

4. in a good sense, prudence, skill, in undertaking and carrying on affairs

New Living Bible But I am afraid that, as the serpent deceived Eve by his craftiness, your minds will be led astray from the simplicity and purity of devotion to Christ.

Genesis 3:1-7 Now the serpent was more crafty than any beast of the field which the Lord God had made. And he said to the woman, "Indeed, has God said, 'You shall not eat from any tree of the garden'?" The woman said to the serpent, From the fruit of the trees of the garden we may eat; but from the fruit of the tree which is in the middle of the garden, God has said, You shall not eat from it or touch it, or you will die. And when the woman saw that the tree was good for food, and that it was pleasant to the eyes, and a tree to be desired to make one wise, she took of the fruit thereof, and did eat, and gave also unto her husband with her; and he did eat. And the eyes of them both were opened, and they knew that they were naked; and they sewed fig leaves together, and made themselves aprons.

Genesis 3:13-15 And the LORD God said unto the woman, What is this that thou hast done? And the woman said, The serpent beguiled me, and I did eat. And the LORD God said unto the serpent, Because thou hast done this, thou art cursed above all cattle, and above every beast of the field; upon thy belly shalt thou go, and dust shalt thou eat all the days of thy life: And I will put enmity between thee and the woman, and between thy seed and her Seed; It shall bruise thy head, and thou shalt bruise His heel.

Proverbs 31:30 Charm is deceptive, and beauty is fleeting, but a woman who fears the Lord is to be praised.

Proverbs 26:24-28 He that hateth dissembleth with his lips, and layeth up deceit within him; When he speaketh fair, believe him not: for there are seven abominations in his heart. Whose hatred is covered by deceit, his wickedness shall be shewed before the whole congregation. Whoso diggeth a pit shall fall therein: and he that rolleth a stone, it will return upon him. A lying tongue hateth those that are afflicted by it; and a flattering mouth worketh ruin.

Deliverance Activation

- Explore this word before God and journal further what God is speaking to you.
- Explore and journal how you can help keep women from falling prey to this attack.

God's Kingdom Women Arise

Word of Revelation released February 27, 2020

God is calling women forth in a grand way in this hour. It is not to dishonor men or negate the need for men, but to honor the servitude, longevity of service and worship, and the seek of women. The women God is SHIFTING forth have God's heart. They are very loyal, strong, powerful, and multifaceted. They are striving to balance the power, calling, and authority on their lives without being viewed negatively or as anti-feminine as a result of how God is using them. It is so important for men to embrace this SHIFT because it disallows the enemy the opportunity to breed misunderstanding, keeping him from causing confusion and deceiving people into believing that women are trying to take the place of men in society and in the body of Christ. Men must be able to make space for and empower these women in order to keep the enemy from presenting it as a feminist movement when it is a God movement.

On the other hand, it will also be important for women to partner with and empower men, honoring their God-given roles biblically and in society while, at the same time, not negating what God is also SHIFTING them forth to do.

Regarding the SHIFT that God is doing in this hour, women must empower and support other women as well so that we will not become a kingdom divided.

Our traditional roles have changed and that is okay. But those who have chosen to maintain traditional roles are still needed and are just as important. Honoring the role and rise of the woman in every fashion is essential to us successfully embracing and sustaining the SHIFT of women who are arising for the glory of God in this hour.

I asked God the reason for women arising in this hour. He said it was not to dishonor men, but that He hoped men would know their identities as coverings, protectors, and providers and that they would SHIFT into position and govern and partner with the women and youth as they SHIFT forth. He then gave me the following word:

"I am honoring the seek of the woman. Women want My Kingdom to come and have been pursuing Me and My Kingdom with great fervor to see My will come to pass in the earth. Women have been carrying My church for the last season and the present season. They have been showing up at church, traveling from conference to conference, pursuing training and equipping, so that they can carry and release My glory in the earth.

I am honoring their dedication and pursuit with kingship and as just judges - as Apostles and apostolic warriors. They shall arise as Deborahs and Davids - as Paul's and Peters. Dismantling the principalities and powers of darkness and cutting off that which is not of Me - SHIFTING in My glory and building My kingdom with fierceness and no regard to trial and persecution. They shall birth Me, nurture Me, cultivate

7

Me, proclaim Me, advance Me, and establish Me with sustaining strength, such that My new blueprint is trailblazer in the earth.

Women are doing the work to become pure and remain pure. They are uncompromising. They have decided that making the necessary sacrifices to be obedient to Me is better than being compromising and misaligned in My will and purpose. They have decided upon themselves that settling is a sin and have rejected the lie and trap that they are defined by what man and society think they should be as women. They are allowing Me to define them and to use their wombs for My glory. They will birth and build with unexplainable tenacity, fruitfulness, and multiplication in this next dispensation because of their willingness to be used of Me and to only want to birth what pleases Me. My hand is indeed upon them - the rib. Even as I have created them to come along the side of the man, they have risen to come under and along the side of Me for Kingdom advancement. I am proud of the woman.

There has been a crying out from the prayer closets of women. They have not been too proud to pursue Me - to humble themselves before. They have been crying out for My church. They have been crying out for the world. They have been crying out for the men and the children. They have been crying out for families and salvation for loved ones. They have been crying out for My hand to SHIFT earth where they experience My daily revival glory and reformation. They have been not just asking but seeking Me - building covenant with Me. They joy, linger, and wait in My presence. They do not leave Me when I do not respond how they think I should. They do not punish Me for not being who they want Me to be. They allow Me to be Me - to be God and they trust Me ultimately even if they do not understand all My decisions and ways. I am honoring them in this season. For it is indeed deserving. They trust Me and I trust them, so I help them produce My will and purpose in the earth.

My calling forth - my arising of women and hand upon the younger is not to negate the men. If anything, it should prick them to SHIFT into position and to cover the seed and queens I have granted to their hands."

Shift!

Deliverance Activation

1. Explore this word before God and journal further what God is speaking to you.
2. Set three goals for how you can SHIFT forth in accomplishing what God is granting to your hands.
3. Journal the reasons this word is significant for this dispensation.
4. Journal how you can honor men, yet still take your rightful place in the earth.
5. Journal the support you need from men and how you can receive support without downgrading yourself, compromising what God is saying, overstepping men, or succumbing to the warlock spirit.

Characteristic Of A Warlock

From my manual "Unmasking The Power Of The Scouts: Soul Stealers."

Types of Warlocks:

Warlock is the name for a male witch. The definition of the word warlock is "path breaker, deceiver, traitor, liar. These definitions are derived from historical acts of foundational warlocks making a pact with the devil, while separating from God and religious practices. I would contend that warlocks are lockers. They lock their prey down and hold them in bondage with their clever powers. Warlocks are very militant and learn and operate in their craft in a very military type of system. The way they learn their trade and operate in their craft requires them to become a master and obtain certain ranks until they reach a level of mastery. As they train and SHIFT through the ranks, they are required to memorize their rituals and spells, thus embodying the works, such that they become the identity of the magic and witchcraft powers they are studying. The intent is to SHIFT to the highest rank of thought magic where they can control and manipulate everything and anything through supernatural powers.

Warlocks craft in the dark arts (manic and spell work used to harm, control, or kill their victim), magic, sorcery, conjuring and necromancy. They are generally called necromancers, pit servers, high priests, witch doctors, shaman, and witches. Extreme warlocks operate in high level witchcraft that include altar worship and rituals, ceremonies, cosmic energy practices, spell casting, astral projection and communing with demonic forces and being in realms and spheres, communing and covenanting with Satan, animal and human blood sacrificing, and sexual and sadistic rituals. The average warlock is overly self-absorbed, egotistical, and some are narcissistic. They pride themselves on being supreme and individualistic in their ideologies and behaviors, and many view those around them as subservient and opportunities to work their craft for the purposes of increasing their warlock rank. Some warlocks are so possessed by demons, they may manifest demonic traits, exhibit inhuman strength, and supernatural behaviors. High level warlocks and witches can operate as shape shifters where they can change their physical form at will or adapt behaviorally to any situation.

A wizard tends to be a male, who operates skillfully in magic, mysticism, magical and mystical practices, or wizardry. Wizards tend to work as illusionists or in positions that allow them to perform acts of trickery and deception on people. Some of them make pacts with demons to perform their wizardry as they aim to be the best at their craft and engage in illusions that present them as masters of their craft. They rarely share their techniques with others because the more individualistic they are, the greater the fame, success, and fortune of their craft.

Warlocks Infiltrating the Church
Warlocks groom their women using their spiritual charisma. They appear spiritual as they use their works to seduce women into their web. Most warlocks do not have an intimate relationship with God and are surface in their walk with God. Saints, especially women, tend to look at

their religious acts or fall for their seductive spiritual jargon when God looks on the heart.

Characteristics of a Church Warlock

- Can be a believer or non-believer.
- Handsome or distinct, unique, and interesting in physical appearance, demeanor, and character.
- Seductively drawing, alluring, mesmerizing.
- Cunning and crafty.
- Use trickery and deception to lure their victim.
- Prey on the innocence and purity of others.
- Seek to steal one's purity and virtuous standing with God.
- Prey on women who desire marriage, insecure in their identity, and anxious in their ability to wait for a mate.
- Some hide amongst the members and search out his or her prey, while others use religious works to draw prey to himself.
- Rushes relationships, to hook his prey.
- Studies their prey so they can war successfully to lock down their soul.
- Use words to curse, lure, cast spells on his prey.
- Gives gifts to flatter and draw prey unto himself.
- Covenant breakers and lack true commitment though may speak otherwise.
- Not truly submitted to leadership, the vision of the ministry, the fellowship, or to people in general; very individualistic in his ideologies and works;

uses this to draw victim into secret encounters and sinful behaviors.

- Self-absorbed but makes others interested in pleasing and engaging him.
- Tend to have two or more personalities; can be charming one minute, angry, violent, and controlling the next.
- Enrages when feels threatened in his manhood.
- Tends to use verbal intimidation, belittling, manipulation, aggression, to steal the victim's identity and self-confidence.
- Poor communicator; insecure, while appearing prideful and overly self-confident; will become aggressive and belittling when misunderstood or when insecurity is exposed.
- Blames inappropriate behaviors on the victim; presents himself as the victim even though he is the offender.
- Soul ties his victim to him then use shame, blame, guilt, false promises and prophecies to keep her locked to him.
- After grooming his victim, isolates them from loved ones, ministry purposes, and the fellowship.
- Victim will begin to experience spiritual, emotional, physical, and financial decline due to being locked down by the warlock, and him draining them of the fruit of their identity and purpose.
- May try to make the victim financially dependent on him or may become financially dependent on the victim, while claim what is theirs as his, and demanding or manipulating the victim to care for him.

- May come from an unhealthy family or life background; is unhealed of these wounds.
- Controlling, very jealous, accusatory, constantly questioning and demanding answers regarding people, whereabouts, and actions.
- Once sex is involved, it soul ties the warlock to the victim. This makes deliverance more difficult. It also further locks the victim in where they have challenges making decisions for themselves.
- Withhold love, sex, communication as punishment or to further lock victim into his control.
- Embarrasses victim in front of others; may contend it was a joke, a misunderstanding, or deserved.
- Makes victim feel as if they are losing their mind and do not trust themselves anymore; victim has lost self and can only be restored until the relationship is severed or the warlock receives personal deliverance and healing.
- May become physically aggressive; will be nice one minute and engaged as if he is another person the next.
- Will refuse intervention from leaders, parents, authority figures; will claim challenges handled without outside interference; this only further isolates the victim and promotes helplessness and hopelessness with breaking free.
- Is bound by the demonic spirits that oppress or possess the warlock since their soul is tied to his; must be free from these spirits to be totally delivered from the warlock experience.

The Craftiness Of Satan

Satan was the first warlock. His craftiness drew Eve from the covering of God and her husband. As she believed his lies, her reactions changed the course of destiny for all mankind.

Remember this statement:

Because women are birthers, what they carry has the potential to impact all of mankind.

The devil knows this all too well. He hates this truth about women. He has always been after the woman's ability to birth, their virtue, and their seed. This is the reason a warlock tends to use a woman or a child when offering a sacrifice to Satan to obtain power, fame, fortune, and success. He especially uses a woman who is a virgin and, of course, we know that children are innocent and virgins as well. The warlock knows that Satan views the woman and her seed as potent valuable sacrifices. He wants the power of their ability to produce and reproduce for himself.

2Corinthians 11:3 But I fear, lest by any means, as the serpent beguiled Eve through his subtilty, so your minds should be corrupted from the simplicity that is in Christ.

Beguiled means *"to deceive and to seduce wholly."*

Subtility is *panourgia* in Greek and means:
1. adroitness (subtle ease and ingenuity)
2. i.e. (in a bad sense) trickery or sophistry: cunning, craftiness, subtilty
3. craftiness, cunning, a specious or false wisdom
4. in a good sense, prudence, skill, in undertaking and carrying on affairs

New Living Bible But I am afraid that, as the serpent deceived Eve by his craftiness, your minds will be led astray from the simplicity and purity of devotion to Christ.

Genesis 3:1-7 Now the serpent was more crafty than any beast of the field which the Lord God had made. And he said to the woman, "Indeed, has God said, 'You shall not eat from any tree of the garden'?" The woman said to the serpent, From the fruit of the trees of the garden we may eat; but from the fruit of the tree which is in the middle of the garden, God has said, You shall not eat from it or touch it, or you will die. And when the woman saw that the tree was good for food, and that it was pleasant to the eyes, and a tree to be desired to make one wise, she took of the fruit thereof, and did eat, and gave also unto her husband with her; and he did eat. And the eyes of them both were opened, and they knew that they were naked; and they sewed fig leaves together, and made themselves aprons.

__Genesis 3:13-15__ And the LORD God said unto the woman, What is this that thou hast done? And the woman said, The serpent beguiled me, and I did eat. And the LORD God said unto the serpent, Because thou hast done this, thou art cursed above all cattle, and above every beast of the field; upon thy belly shalt thou go, and dust shalt thou eat all the days of thy life: And I will put enmity between thee and the woman, and between thy seed and her Seed; It shall bruise thy head, and thou shalt bruise His heel.

The enemy wants to cause when to stray from their foundation in God. He wants them to be uprooted so that the power of their purity and ability to birth through a pure well will be tainted by the illegal open womb that manifests when they seek knowledge, pleasure, and purpose, outside of the boundaries of God. He knows that within the boundaries of God, the woman can crush his head, and continue to birth head crushers that annihilate his kingdom.

The enemy preys on a woman's inquisition. Truth is, Eve had all the revelation she needed. The serpent created in her, a desire to know beyond what was necessary for her life. She was then unable to remain guarded in the true word God, that protected her, her husband, her seed, and all of mankind.

This is the work of a warlock. The woman will know truth, but the craftiness of the warlock's operation creates an inquisition to know and pursue beyond truth. When that boundary is crossed, the hooking of the warlock begins.

Deliverance Activation

- Journal your thoughts on the power of women being birthers.
- Journal how Satan has an assault on the identity and womb of women.

The Hooking Lock

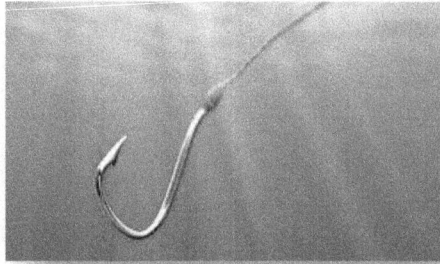

There are two words that make up the word -
warlock. Those words are "War" and "Lock."

Dictionary.com defined *war* as:
1. active hostility or contention; conflict; contest
2. a conflict carried on by force of arms, as between
   nations or between parties within a nation; warfare, as
   by land, sea, or air
3. a state or period of armed hostility or active military
   operations
4. aggressive business conflict, as through severe price
   cutting in the same industry or any other means of
   undermining competitors
5. a battle
6. a struggle to achieve a goal
7. to make or carry on war; fight
8. to be in conflict or in a state of strong opposition

Dictionary.com defines *lock* as:
1. a device for securing a door, gate, lid, drawer, or the
   like in position when closed, consisting of a bolt or
   system of bolts propelled and withdrawn by a
   mechanism operated by a key, dial, etc.

2. a contrivance for fastening or securing something
    (in a firearm) the mechanism that explodes the charge;
    gunlock
3. (in safety) any device or part for stopping temporarily
    the motion of a mechanism
4. complete and unchallenged control; an unbreakable
    hold

A warlock is always at war with what is of God. The warlock seeks to hook a person and then lock them in under his prison of control. Initially when the locking occurs, the person hooked in may experience a sense of security, protection, and regard for being in the intimate or secure space of the warlock. The warlock will make the person believe this is a sacred space and they should be honored to be there. As the person becomes comfortable, vulnerable, susceptible, unguarded in their perceptions and behaviors, reliant and relinquishing of control to the warlock, the person then enters a war between striving to honor the demands, controls, manipulations, and seductions of the warlock and honoring the truth of God's standards, will, and purpose for his or her life.

When people are warlocked in, there may be several wars going on in and around them. Those wars may be as follows:

✓ The war between their flesh and their spirit,
   especially if an emotional or sexual soul tie has
   been formed.

✓ A war in their soul as the warlock has soul tied the
   person to them and any demonic spirits that are
   oppressing the warlock.

✓ The war between them and the warlock, especially if there is a difference between morals, values, and standards.

✓ A war between God and the devil for the person's soul and salvation.

Mental and psychological warfare as the person is striving to navigate through the bewitchment and confusion that has come from being under the warlock's hooking control.

- *Mental Warfare* (Discombobulated, reduced, or altered in the mind, emotions, thoughts, senses)

- *Psychological Warfare* (Discombobulated, reduced, or altered in morale, abilities, capabilities, identity, comprehension, worth, value, strength, stamina)

Mental and psychological warfare from territorial spirits and principalities in the person's region who are using this situation as an open door to further oppress, depress, and bewitch the person; this occurs and is strengthened through bewitching words, manipulations, and curses released by the warlock. Territorial spirits pick these words and conversations up on the frequencies and airways around the person and begin using then to cause further trauma and bondage that hooks them into the situation and makes it difficult to break free from the relationship. The mental warfare will cause constant thought racing, dejection, defeat, depression, confusing, mind binding, and entanglement. The person will have a difficult time receiving truth and making correct decisions that are best for their lives and well-being.

Once locked in, there is usually something significant about the person's life, calling, virtue, standards that the warlock uses to further manipulate, bewitch, and hook the person into his control. The warlock knows that this is what gives that person their uniqueness and sets them apart. He wants the person to devalue and compromise it, so the person loses their power and significance allowing the warlock to gain the power, virtue, and authority of what has now been surrendered under his control.

Acts 8:14-24 The Amplified Bible Now when the apostles (special messengers) at Jerusalem heard that [the country of] Samaria had accepted and welcomed the Word of God, they sent Peter and John to them, And they came down and prayed for them that the Samaritans might receive the Holy Spirit; For He had not yet fallen upon any of them, but they had only been baptized into the name of the Lord Jesus. Then [the apostles] laid their hands on them one by one, and they received the Holy Spirit.

However, when Simon saw that the [Holy] Spirit was imparted through the laying on of the apostles' hands, he brought money and offered it to them, Saying, Grant me also this power and authority, in order that anyone on whom I place my hands may receive the Holy Spirit. But Peter said to him, Destruction overtake your money and you, because you imagined you could obtain the [free] gift of God with money!

You have neither part nor lot in this matter, for your heart is all wrong in God's sight [it is not straightforward or right or true before God]. So repent of this depravity and wickedness of yours and pray to the Lord that, if possible, this contriving thought and purpose of your heart may be

22

removed and disregarded and forgiven you. For I see that you are in the gall of bitterness and in a bond forged by iniquity [to fetter souls]. And Simon answered, Pray for me [beseech the Lord, both of you], that nothing of what you have said may befall me!

In this passage we see Simon so intrigued by the Holy Spirit's power and ability to impart it into others that he wanted to purchase it. He did not realize that it was a sacred, free gift given by God. This is the character of a warlock. They are drawn to your anointing and the uniqueness of the Holy Spirit in you that they want to own as they recognize the power of it in you. They have no idea what it cost you to govern it nor do they realize that it was freely given simply because you are you. They will do whatever it takes to charm you, thus purchasing your love and your trust, so they can lock in your most valuable asset that God has deemed sacred about you.

Acts 8:21-23 King James Bible *Thou hast neither part nor lot in this matter: for thy heart is not right in the sight of God. Repent therefore of this thy wickedness, and pray God, if perhaps the thought of thine heart may be forgiven thee. For I perceive that thou art in the gall of bitterness, and in the bond of iniquity.*

Peter did not have any compromise or grace for Simon. He did not give Simon a chance to make excuses for his actions nor give him an opportunity to charm his way out of the truth that was being revealed about his character and motives. Peter blatantly told Simon that his heart was not right before God and that he needed to repent for his wickedness. Peter expressed further that he discerned a wicked root, bitter fruit, and a bond with iniquity. *Adikia* is

23

the Greek work for *iniquity* and means *"sin, wrongfulness, unrighteousness, and violating laws and deeds of justice."*

Often when the person being hooked in confronts the warlock, the warlock is given an opportunity to talk their way out of what the person is discerning. The warlock makes the person feel that what they are perceiving is untrue and is a misunderstanding. Even though the person has a strong warning, they will yield to the warlock's gaslighting. The gaslighting causes the person to doubt their truth and sanity through the use of psychological manipulation. The more gas lighting is used, the stronger the warlock hook becomes. The person cannot imagine or see their life without the person as their entire identity becomes suppressed under the warlock's control.

Peter was not falling for Simon's hook. He judged Simon immediately and encouraged him to repent. This is how a person should engage in war with a warlock. However, because of the manner to which the warlock operates, the person ends up being the one repenting and feeling sorrowful for their actions as they are made to feel as though they judged the warlock unjustly. Such deceitful manipulation reveals just how locked in a person may be. The person will know they are in trouble and imprisoned by the warlock but feel helpless to break free from their charm and deception.

Proverbs 31:30 *Charm is deceptive, and beauty is fleeting, but a woman who fears the Lord is to be praised.*

In this passage of scripture, the woman is told not to use charm as deceit. It is interesting that charm would also come through the tactics of the warlock to hook the woman.

Proverbs 26:24-28 *He that hateth dissembleth with his lips, and layeth up deceit within him; When he speaketh fair, believe him not: for there are seven abominations in his heart. Whose hatred is covered by deceit, his wickedness shall be shewed before the whole congregation. Whoso diggeth a pit shall fall therein: and he that rolleth a stone, it will return upon him. A lying tongue hateth those that are afflicted by it; and a flattering mouth worketh ruin.*

Deceit is *mirmâ* in Hebrew and means, "in the sense of deceiving; fraud, craft, deceit(-ful, -fully), false, feigned, guile, subtilly, treachery."

The seven abominations are listed in *Proverbs 6:16-19*:

These six things doth the Lord hate: yea, seven are an abomination unto him: A proud look, a lying tongue, and hands that shed innocent blood, An heart that deviseth wicked imaginations, feet that be swift in running to mischief, A false witness that speaketh lies, and he that soweth discord among brethren.

The Lord Hates

1. **A proud look** - any person, ideology, perception, or behavior that is lifted up above God.

2. **Lying tongue** - any deceitful, wrongful, false, vain, bogus, pretentious effort to draw someone away from what pleases, honors, and edifies God.

3. **Hands that shed innocent blood** - any attempt to spiritually or natural murder or kill someone with words or deeds; kill their destiny, identity, progress, process, success, purity, innocence, virtue in and with God.

4. **Hearts that devise wicked imaginations** - any effort to cause affliction, mischief, iniquity, or sorrow through decisive and manipulative schemes and acts; or curious workings which biblically means witchcraft and bewitchment.

5. **Feet swift in running to mischief** - moving quickly, hastily, and cunningly, where there is no time to make proper decisions or detect wrongdoing, wretchedness, ill-intent or affliction.

6. **False witness that speak lies** - twisting the truth, telling half-truths, and/or spreading lies, to make the victim look like the offender - the aggressor - the predator; keeping records of wrong then using them to justify gaslighting and wrongdoings being held accountable for one's actions.

7. **He that sows discord** - gaslighting or causing strife, contention, and conflict, where offense and confusion

overrides the ability to discern truth and resolve conflict in a godly manner.

The Amplified Bible He who hates pretends with his lips, but stores up deceit within himself. When he speaks kindly, do not trust him, for seven abominations are in his heart. Though his hatred covers itself with guile, his wickedness shall be shown openly before the assembly. Whoever digs a pit [for another man's feet] shall fall into it himself, and he who rolls a stone [up a height to do mischief], it will return upon him. A lying tongue hates those it wounds and crushes, and a flattering mouth works ruin.

The Amplified Bible says that even when this person speaks kindly, do not fall for it, for seven abominations are within him waiting to be unleashed. No matter how sexy and flattering those lips are, when Holy Spirit in you is saying, "He is a pretender," trust Holy Spirit. Seek wise counsel before you dismiss your Holy Spirit unction. The Message Bible says that once you yield, bruh is waiting to rip you off.

RIP OFF YOUR DESTINY!

The Message Bible Your enemy shakes hands and greets you like an old friend, all the while conniving against you. When he speaks warmly to you, don't believe him for a minute; he's just waiting for the chance to rip you off. No matter how cunningly he conceals his malice, eventually his evil will be exposed in public. Malice backfires; spite boomerangs. Liars hate their victims; flatterers sabotage trust.

Shift!

Deliverance Activation

1. Spend time asking God to identify past and present pretenders in your life. Journal what he shares. Ask Him to increase your discernment so that you can identify pretenders quickly.

2. Search out any open doors in your life that would be subject to opening the door to pretenders. Work with God to close those doors and practice keeping them closed until this becomes a normal standard in your life.

3. Spend time studying the seven abominations and asking God how they would seek to operate in your life.

4. Examine any present and past relationships and identify any way you have succumbed to the charm and pretentious ways of a person and how it resulted in opening the doors to the seven abominations.

5. Spend time breaking free from every soul tie to past pretenders and any way you are warlocked under their seven abominations.

6. Ask God to judge and expose any warlock assignments against your life and destiny. Spend time in spiritual warfare breaking these assignments, hooks, and lickings, personally and generationally off your life.

Unintentional Warlock Workings

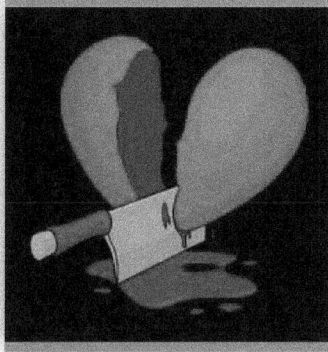

Sometimes a woman can have a warlock experience without actually encountering a full-blown warlock. Let's explore the instances in which this can occur.

Unbeliever

The person may not be saved at all, but a good guy; he may not be a godly guy, or the guy God has for you.

2Corinthians 6:14-18 Do not be unequally yoked with unbelievers [do not make mismated alliances with them or come under a different yoke with them, inconsistent with your faith]. For what partnership have right living and right standing with God with iniquity and lawlessness? Or how can light have fellowship with darkness? What harmony can there be between Christ and Belial [the devil]? Or what has a believer in common with an unbeliever? What agreement [can there be between] a temple of God and idols? For we are the temple of the living God; even as God said, I will dwell in and with and among them and will walk in and with and among them, and I will be their God, and they shall be My people. So,

*come out from among [unbelievers], and separate (sever)
yourselves from them, says the Lord, and touch not [any]
unclean thing; then I will receive you kindly and treat you
with favor, And will be a Father unto you, and ye shall be
my sons and daughters, saith the Lord Almighty.*

Claim Salvation

The person may claim salvation, but may not be delivered,
healed, or striving to live a sanctified life of holiness.

*Romans 6:1-2 What shall we say, then? Shall we go on
sinning so that grace may increase? By no means! We are
those who have died to sin; how can we live in it any
longer?*

*Romans 6:6 For we know that our old self was crucified
with him so that the body ruled by sin might be done away
with, that we should no longer be slaves to sin because
anyone who has died has been set free from sin.*

*1John 3:8-10 Whoever makes a practice of sinning is of the
devil, for the devil has been sinning from the beginning.
The reason the Son of God appeared was to destroy the
works of the devil. No one born of God makes a practice of
sinning, for God's seed abides in him, and he cannot keep
on sinning because he has been born of God. By this it is
evident who are the children of God, and who are the
children of the devil: whoever does not practice
righteousness is not of God, nor is the one who does not
love his brother.*

Backsliders

This person may not be grounded in God, backsliding into sin. Backsliders tend to operate in the spirit of the crab where they pull others down in a backsliding state with them. This makes the backslider and open doors to operating in warlock behavior.

Matthew 13:20-21 The seed falling on rocky ground refers to someone who hears the word and at once receives it with joy. But since they have no root, they last only a short time. When trouble or persecution comes because of the word, they quickly fall away.

Soul Wounds

The person may have some hurts and traumas. He may not know how to govern his soul, less known, engage you in a healthy God-fearing, God-led relationship.

1John 2:19 They went out from us, but they did not really belong to us. For if they had belonged to us, they would have remained with us; but their going showed that none of them belonged to us.

Hebrews 6:4-6 It is impossible for those who have once been enlightened, who have tasted the heavenly gift, who have shared in the Holy Spirit, who have tasted the goodness of the word of God and the powers of the coming age and who have fallen away, to be brought back to repentance. To their loss they are crucifying the Son of God all over again and subjecting him to public disgrace.

2Peter 2:20-21 If they have escaped the corruption of the world by knowing our Lord and Savior Jesus Christ and are again entangled in it and are overcome, they are worse off at the end than they were at the beginning. It would have been better for them not to have known the way of righteousness, than to have known it and then to turn their backs on the sacred command that was passed on to them.

God's Permissive Will - Ishmaels

The person may be dealing with his own hope deferred issues and view you as an opportunity to manipulate his divine promises into fusion. This is more like one's permissive will at work or an Ishmael situation, where the person implements their own will to produce fruit. The people around this person are manipulated so that plan B manifests plan-A fruit. You are hooked into the entanglement to meet a need and desire at the expense of your own purity, destiny, and progress. Study the story of Abraham, Sarah, and Hagar in Genesis 16-18. Sarah encouraged Abraham to use Hagar to produce a child for them. Hagar was their handmaiden, so she was already at their mercy. Hagar was eventually asked to leave with the child as if she was the one who schemed the warlock situation.

The Deceitful Church Goer

The person may be a church leader, worship leader, musician, deacon, dedicated church goer that attends all the ministry services and events. They may attend conferences and convocation, while presenting all the forms of a godly man, yet underneath, the warlock is brooding.

2Corinthians 11:13-14 For such are false apostles, deceitful workers, transforming themselves into the apostles of Christ. And no marvel; for Satan himself is transformed into an angel of light. Therefore, it is no great thing if his ministers also be transformed as the ministers of righteousness; whose end shall be according to their works.

John 8:44-45 *Ye are of your father the devil, and the lusts of your father ye will do. He was a murderer from the beginning, and abode not in the truth, because there is no truth in him. When he speaketh a lie, he speaketh of his own: for he is a liar, and the father of it. And because I tell you the truth, ye believe me not.*

Matthew 7:21-23 *Not everyone who says to Me, Lord, Lord! will enter the kingdom of heaven, but only the one who does the will of My Father in heaven. On that day many will say to Me, Lord, Lord, didn't we prophesy in Your name, drive out demons in Your name, and do many miracles in Your name? Then I will announce to them, I never knew you! Depart from Me, you lawbreakers!*

Jude 1:3-4 The Amplified Bible *Beloved, my whole concern was to write to you in regard to our common salvation. [But] I found it necessary and was impelled to write you and urgently appeal to and exhort [you] to contend for the faith which was once for allhanded down to the saints [the faith which is that sum of Christian belief which was delivered verbally to the holy people of God]. For certain men have crept in stealthily [gaining entrance secretly by a side door]. Their doom was predicted long ago, ungodly (impious, profane) persons who pervert the grace (the spiritual blessing and favor) of our God into lawlessness and wantonness and immorality, and disown*

33

and deny our sole Master and Lord, Jesus Christ (the Messiah, the Anointed One).

Perversion & Open Doors

The person may have some perversions, lust, and open doors that causes him to operate in warlock behavior.

***Matthew 5:28** But I say unto you, That whosoever looketh on a woman to lust after her hath committed adultery with her already in his heart.*

David, a man after God's own heart, warlocked Bathsheba. To cover his workings, he contrived to have her husband killed in war. Though this was a cover up in the natural, it did not get past God. God sees all and made David accountable for his actions.

***2Samuel 11:2-5** And it came to pass in an eveningtide, that David arose from off his bed, and walked upon the roof of the king's house: and from the roof he saw a woman washing herself; and the woman was very beautiful to look upon. And David sent and enquired after the woman. And one said, Is not this Bathsheba, the daughter of Eliam, the wife of Uriah the Hittite? And David sent messengers, and took her; and she came in unto him, and he lay with her; for she was purified from her uncleanness: and she returned unto her house. And the woman conceived, and sent and told David, and said, I am with child.*

David Enquired of naked Bathsheba who was minding her own business as she bathed in her roof. *Enquired* in the Hebrew means *"inquisition."* Instead of going back in the house to his own wife, he opened the door in wanting to know - inquire - about another man's wife beyond God's boundary line. David was not trying the be a warlock. He loved God, was a God seeker, yet allowed his eyes to draw him into behavior unbecoming of a godly king. Bathsheba was prey without even knowing it. She most likely felt obligated to fulfilled David's request because of his position as king.

How many women succumb to the warlock of their leader out of obligation. Add flattery and fascination to the mix and the warlock hook has imprisoned its prey?

David and Bathsheba had a child that died as a result of their sin. How many women in the church have had to endure the shame and consequences of the warlocking of their leaders? (*Study 2Samuel 11-12*).

Familiar Spirits & Generational Strongholds

Familiar spirits & generational strongholds can be an intentional or unintentional warlock working. Sometimes we are not discerning of how familiar spirits operate from generation to generation in our family line. Or how familiar spirits follow us from relationship to relationship to bind and sabotage our progress and destiny. It is important to be discerning regarding the relationships, cycles, and patterns that the women and couples within the family have experienced. Patterns of abuse, neglect, divorce, singleness, having children out of wedlock, unhealthy and ungodly relationships, failure to maintain relationships, are telling signs of familiar spirits and generational curses are in operation. When these spirits cannot rule in the natural realm of women, they may attack sexually and physically via dreams or as the women sleep at night. Breaking curses and closing generational doorways and portals connected to sin, iniquity, idolatry, and witchcraft is key to breaking these attacks, nullifying curses, and casting out familiar spirits.

Leviticus 19:31 Regard not them that have familiar spirits, neither seek after wizards, to be defiled by them: I am the LORD your God.

Isaiah 8:19 And when they shall say unto you, Seek unto them that have familiar spirits, and unto wizards that peep, and that mutter: should not a people seek unto their God? for the living to the dead?

Leviticus 20:6 And the soul that turneth after such as have familiar spirits, and after wizards, to go a whoring after them, I will even set my face against that soul, and will cut him off from among his people.

Deuteronomy 18:10 There shall not be found among you any one that maketh his son or his daughter to pass through the fire, or that useth divination, or an observer of times, or an enchanter, or a witch,

2Chronicles 33:6 And he caused his children to pass through the fire in the valley of the son of Hinnom: also he observed times, and used enchantments, and used witchcraft, and dealt with a familiar spirit, and with wizards: he wrought much evil in the sight of the LORD, to provoke him to anger.

2Kings 21:6 And he made his son pass through the fire, and observed times, and used enchantments, and dealt with familiar spirits and wizards: he wrought much wickedness in the sight of the LORD, to provoke him to anger.

__Psalms 91:5__ Thou shalt not be afraid for the terror by night; nor for the arrow that flieth by day;

Warlock Trauma

I would assert that these experiences are more concerning than the blatant warlock because it requires keen discernment to avoid its entanglement. A few major inquisitions that cause women to get caught up is the need to:

- ✓ Fix the man
- ✓ Take the man on as a salvation or deliverance project
- ✓ Save the man
- ✓ Shape and mold the man into what they want him to be or think they should be

All these areas are inquisitions of potential rather than operating in the truth and reality of that person.

Potential is:

- Possible, as opposed to actual
- Capable of being or becoming Expressing possibility
- A latent excellence or ability that may or may not be developed

Reality is:

- The state or quality of being real
- Resemblance to what is real
- A real thing or fact; factual

- The actual truth of what is real; authentic

There is nothing wrong with potential as long as the person is actually demonstrating that they are working towards realization. When there is no true working and just a lot of talk and empty promises, you may very well be encountering a pretender.

Proverbs 26:24-28 He that hateth dissembleth with his lips, and layeth up deceit within him; When he speaketh fair, believe him not: for there are seven abominations in his heart. Whose hatred is covered by deceit, his wickedness shall be shewed before the whole congregation. Whoso diggeth a pit shall fall therein: and he that rolleth a stone, it will return upon him. A lying tongue hateth those that are afflicted by it; and a flattering mouth worketh ruin.

Proverbs 6:16-19 These six things doth the Lord hate: yea, seven are an abomination unto him: A proud look, a lying tongue, and hands that shed innocent blood, An heart that deviseth wicked imaginations, feet that be swift in running to mischief, A false witness that speaketh lies, and he that soweth discord among brethren.

This person may not even be aware they are a pretender or that those seven abominations are in them ready to work you over. They just keep making promise after promise, while encouraging you to trust them and give them a chance. There is minimal to no fruit to show that they are actually striving to align with, become, and do what God says. Potential will have you making excuses for the lack of productivity in the person's life. The soul tie will have you agreeing to the imprisonment of the false realities of the person's life.

Many women delay ending the relationship because they dread being embarrassed for relenting to potential. Amid their delay the fixer spirit within them SHIFTs into full effect. They literally become God in the man's life as they go on fasts, consecrations, engage in manipulating Intercessory prayers that I contend is failed bewitchment, while striving to get the man to commit to goals and behaviors that he often does not keep. The man then begins to use the woman's erred actions as ammunition to make her look like the witch in the relationship. There is some truth to this as the woman's tactics are an effort to lock the warlock into her web. This results in contention as the warlock behaviors in the man and the witching behaviors in the woman begin to combat against one another.

Regardless of whether they stay together or the break up, both are losers. The relationship is not rooted in Godly acts and principles, so staying together or breaking up results in contentious trauma drama interactions as they have done nothing but abused, manipulated, and afflicted one another.

- ✓ Some women remain in these relationships for years before they realize what they have succumb too.

- ✓ Some women are traumatized by a relationship they experienced years ago due to the shock of what they encountered, how they behaved, and how the relationship ended.

Deliverance Activation

1. Journal ways in which you have encountered and/or succumbed to unintentional warlock workings. Journal what you learned about yourself and ways to make responsible decisions in future interactions.

2. If you discern a pattern, journal what is revealed. Spend time closing personal and generational doors and breaking these warlock assignments off your life.

Warlock Through Vision Endeavors

As God releases great visions for businesses, ministries, and organizations to women, they have been in need of training, equipping, investors, partners, encouragers. It is important to note that women do not mind being trained and educated so they can become sufficient in what they are to do and be in life. Statistics reveal that women are receiving degrees at alarming rates. They also eagerly attend conferences, online courses, and pursue continuing education courses to further educate themselves in particular areas. As women are SHIFTING forth in releasing their visions and blueprints in the earth, they have needed the support of men, especially in ministry and in the business arenas, as these have been spheres of influence that men have ruled and dominated.

One challenge that women have faced is the warlocking through vision endeavors. Instead of men getting behind or coming along side of women to help build and support their vision, many men have been pretenders. Many men have offered empty promises and false hopes. Once getting the woman excited about how they will help, many men start to suggest different plans and ventures that blatantly steal the woman's vision plan, or gives the man the rights, credit, glory, rewards, and financial fruit, while the woman does all the work and is pushed to the background, left with nothing. The plans and ventures are presented as in the woman's best interest, the best interest of her vision, and as if she cannot be successful unless she agrees to this plan. If the woman rejects the man's offer, many men stop assisting the woman altogether, while sometimes cutting off all communication and ties. There is usually no communication regarding what happened or the reason this occurred. And if there is communication, it is presented as if the woman did something wrong or was the one who broke ties or the partnership. But the reality is that she was abandoned due to deciding not to accept the alternate plan.

If the woman agrees to the alternate vision, her true vision is usually stolen and altered. It may be given a new name and a few minor changes to make it appear as if it has been perfected to a greater measure. This manipulating tactic is done in hopes that the woman does not realize she has been hoodwinked by pretender. If she tries to reclaim her vision or suggest plans to assist with the vision, she is treated as if she is usurping boundaries or as if her suggestions are not in the best interest of the vision. None of these inferences are true. What has really happened is the woman's vision has been imprisoned by a warlock.

As women arise in their destiny and calling, they need to be mindful of this type of warlocking. I do want to assert that though this occurs with men, it can also happen with strong dominating women as well. My suggestion is not to focus on the gender but seek to be discerning of the operation of this spirit.

It is the virtue and the ability to produce and reproduce that the warlock wants. He knows the power of the vision of a woman and her ability to birth forth to impact the earth. When he placed his seed inside her vision, the birthing and its fruit multiplies. The faster and bigger the vision grows, the greater his power and dominion to rule in the earth.

This is the reason God created man and women to be married and covenant together. He knew the power it produced personally and generationally. When this covenant is bonded in error, the identity and calling of the woman becomes sacrificed. The systematic demonic oppression of the warlock is knitted to the vision, and births in generations, tainting the purity and righteousness of God, and the vision's ability to fulfill God's kingdom mandate. Women must recognize the trickery and deception that resides beneath the warlock pretending to care and help, when truly, he only wants to use her to rule in the place of God in her life, in her vision, and in who she is to be in the earth. What should have been expansion for God, becomes the devil reigning.

Many leaders in the body of Christ who have been mandated to train, equip, and release people in their destinies and callings, have succumbed to using these types of warlock hookings. It has been my experience that many of these leaders tend to have:

- ✓ Soul wounds or unresolved trauma
- ✓ Open doors to greed and fame
- ✓ Big visions and view smaller, similar visions as an opportunity for expansion
- ✓ Clear vision but do not want to do the work; they use the vulnerabilities of young pioneers by presenting plans of aide, when really their intentions are to take over their vision and claim them as their own.

The promise and desire for covenant, spiritual parenting, and validation, cause many pioneering visionaries to become victims of these warlockings. Many times, they do

43

not realize what has occurred until they have already been locked in. By then, they are striving to decipher how a believer could do this to them, how it happened, and how they can break free from it without being labeled as a dishonoring covenant-breaking troublemaker. Women are often labeled as Jezebels or witches. For fear of being mislabeled, many leave quietly without confronting their warlocking leader, without being healed of trauma caused by that leader, and without reclaiming what was stolen or what they invested to be assisted with their vision. They must resort to cutting their loses and moving on, while often watching the warlocking leader reel in their next prey.

As women arise to release their vision, they must be discerning in who to connect to. It is important to:

- Resist moving too quickly

- Reject moving without direction from God

- Reject operating past God's ordained purpose for the relationship

- Reject making excuses for the leader displaying poor character flaws, possessing a lack of follow through, and presenting with inconsistencies with fulfilling promises and business tasks

- Reject questioning their discernment when the Holy Spirit reveal deceptions, trickery, and underlying schemes to them

- Reject wanting covering, connection, and assistance, more than they want to protect the vision

of God from predators or wounded believers who
have open doors to the warlock spirit

God says, *"Trust Me with your vision endeavors. Trust
Me with the blueprint I have given you. Trust me to:*

- ✓ *Give you the wisdom to release it.*
- ✓ *Reveal further wisdom and witty ideals as you are
  obedient to what I have already told you.*
- ✓ *Fund the vision and supply every need.*
- ✓ *Provide partners, covenants, support pillars, and
  investors.*
- ✓ *Bring every word to pass - every word, small and
  great - fulfilling the mandate with glory, honor,
  and overflow.*

- ✓ *Trust Me when you can't see Me.*
- ✓ *Trust Me when you are unsure of yourself and the
  vision.*
- ✓ *Trust Me and know that I reward the faithful and
  will bring every word to pass concerning you.*

*Your trust in Me provides protection against the
warlock. It keeps you from making decisions outside of
My will. Anyone who is truly sent by Me will not rush
you, try to get you to make decisions without Me, will
want you to disobey or dishonor Me. Even when there
are risks and leaps of faith needed, they will not
manipulate or deceive you into making them. They will
want you to be secure in knowing that I am in the moves
and SHIFTS you are taking.*

Trust Me and allow your trust to be a glory shield around the visions I have given you," says the Lord!

Shift!

Deliverance Activation

Spend time allowing God to deliver and heal you from warlocking through vision endeavors:

- Forgive those that warlocked you.

- Forgive yourself for falling to their warlocking.

- Break soul ties, vows, and covenants made with them and made regarding the vision.

- Break the bewitching and hooking off your mind, heart, and soul; and off your vision.

- Spend time warring over your vision and reclaiming it as yours, spiritually and naturally.

- Use the blood of Jesus Christ and the fire of the Holy Spirit; cleanse their demonic seeds, roots, and fruit out of your life and out of your vision.

- Study the story of Laban and Jacob in the Bible and journal what you learned about warlocking through vision endeavors.

- Journal how you were warlocked. Set three to five goals you can implement to avoid this occurring again.

- Ask God for how to proceed regarding the relationship with the warlock and with the vision; Be obedient to what He says.

- Seek wise counsel if you need further clarity and direction on how to proceed.

- Practice trusting God with your destiny and the vision as a lifestyle.

- Get someone who can hold you accountable to only making decisions as God leads.

If you have never experienced this before:

- Study the story of Laban and Jacob in the Bible and journal what you learned about warlocking through vision endeavors.

- Set three to five goals so that you do not succumb to this experience.

- Journal any fears, open doors, or propensities you have regarding yourself as a vision carrier and you have about the vision. Ask God to deliver, heal, and close doors in these areas

- Set three to five goals you can implement to avoid being warlocked in this area.

47

- Practice trusting God with your destiny and the vision as a lifestyle.

- Get you someone who can hold you accountable to only making decisions as God leads.

Characteristics Of A Kingdom Woman

Written By: Evangelist Mercedes Carr
Founder of Be Thou Made Whole Ministry

In today's society, being acknowledged as a "Woman of God" has become a popular element of the Christian culture. Many women identify themselves as God's kingdom queens, but it is essential to make sure we SHIFT beyond what culture identifies as a godly woman, into embodying this identity biblically.

God is calling for the true women of God to arise and display His holiness, righteousness, and standard in the earth. No longer can we sit on the sidelines silently hoping that the women of the next generation will somehow "find their way." The systems of this world are quickly diminishing the value of purity, modesty, and virtue that God ordained us to walk in. It is time that we take our place and operate in the fullness of who God destined us to be in the earth.

The term "Woman of God" refers to a woman who is devout in her belief in God and submitted to His will and plan for her life. A Woman of God has made the commitment of laying down her life for the sake of serving God, serving others, and establishing God's kingdom on earth.

The word "*of*" means:
1. expressing the relationship between a scale or measure of value
2. expressing the relationship between a part and a whole

The first mark of a Woman of God is one who measures her inherent worth, dignity, and value, in relation to Christ. Her scale is not sifted, tipped, or dictated by the standards of this world, but she is firmly planted in the process of transformation through God. A Woman of God is one who knows that she cannot live in her entirety outside of him.

Romans 12:2 *Do not conform to the pattern of this world, but be transformed by the renewing of your mind. Then you will be able to test and approve what God's will is—his good, pleasing and perfect will.*

A Woman of God is an avid learner of God's word and a student of God's presence. She lives in a place of constant renewal because she makes the time to seek God in all things; she allows Him to work in and through her. Prayer and restoration through God's Word are her lifeline and are vital to her identity and purpose. She does not conform to the world; she is determined to change the things that do not bring God glory, honor, or that do not align with His nature.

Let's just pause and take a *Selah* pondering breath on that revelation for a moment.

Women of God, it is your due diligence and mandate to push against conformity. You must walk in continual transformation by submitting your mind to Christ. As society continues to push agendas and mindsets regarding what a Godly woman should look like we must be bound only to God's word and standard for womanhood. The perfect will of God is accessible and attainable for us, but we must first be grounded in God's word in order to hear and discern the voice of God. We must resist the urge to bow to or follow another god or system. As Godly women, we are mandated by God as the standard and the leaders to pave the way in the earth. As we consider the areas where God is requiring us to rise up and lead in biblical womanhood, let's take a moment to define **what a Woman of God is not**.

- A woman of God is not a physical representation of beauty who lacks true Godly substance.
- A woman of God does not operate in feminist theories or in the idea that woman is better than man.
- A woman of God is not defined by her independence, accomplishments, or perceived strength outside of God.
- A woman of God is not dictated or defined by her relationship status.
- A woman of God does not foolishly shrink to the standards and ideologies of this world.
- A woman of God does not find her power in her lack of submission to God.

As we discern the truth regarding what is of God and what is not, we will find that many of the attributes we have coined as "Godliness" are nothing more than religious mindsets and ideologies that are void of God's true virtue and essence. If you grew up in any type of religious community, you may have been told that Women of God must wear long skirts, remain quiet and docile, walk in purity with no knowledge or understanding of how to do it, and blindly follow whatever is being taught and established as truth. Although modesty is essential, purity is biblical, and wisdom is needed, God never intended for the woman to be silent or follow a standard that speaks to the outward appearance without dealing with the inward character. Living a life governed by rules with no true communion with the Spirit of God or an understanding of His reasonings is merely operating in a form of Godliness. This lacks true substance and power and only keeps us in the cycle of performing, in attempts to walk out our godly identity rather than truly embodying it.

2Timothy 3:5-7 Having a form of godliness, but denying the power thereof: from such turn away.

It is essential to SHIFT from walking in forms of godliness in an effort to preserve a standard that God never created for us in the first place. As we reject godliness, we must seek to embody God's true power. It is the spirit of God that gives us the strength to walk in virtue, purity, and righteousness as we are called to do.

1Timothy 6:11 But you, man of God, flee from all this, and pursue righteousness, godliness, faith, love, endurance and gentleness.

Philippians 4:8 Finally, brothers and sisters, whatever is true, whatever is noble, whatever is right, whatever is pure, whatever is lovely, whatever is admirable—if anything is excellent or praiseworthy—think about such things.

As we consider our unique identity blueprint as the women of God, we must live inside and pursue the things God deems good and acceptable. The Godly woman is not led by her heart, but by scripture. We are not seeking to embody standards that are merely popular or accepted by others, but standards that embody truth.

Deliverance Activation

Take a moment to ask yourself these questions as you evaluate your own standards and mindsets of being a Godly woman. Explain your answers.

1. Does your standard align with God's word and does it support His truth?
2. Is your standard playing it safe rather than truly embodying the high moral status that God is calling you to?
3. Does your standard embody purity in mind, body, soul, and spirit and not just the outward appearance?
4. Is your standard deemed admirable by God?
5. Is your standard based on the world's approval?
6. Does your standard require you to operate in the excellency of God?

A Godly woman takes the time and effort to inventory these areas and make sure that she is consistently aligning with the will of God. There are instances where you may have to revisit standards and expectations from previous seasons and allow God to refine you into who He is calling you to be for this moment and season in your life. Being a Godly woman requires upkeep and commitment to submitting in these areas and making changes when necessary.

Proverbs 16:3 *Commit your work to the LORD, and your plans will be established.*

An important element of walking in the fullness of the identity of a Woman of God is being one who commits to the Lord.

The word "*commit*" means, "*to dedicate, devote, pledge, or bind.*"

A woman of God is not simply one who agrees to the work of the Lord, but she has willingly bound her life and pledged her allegiance to Christ. With this act of commitment and submission to God, He is able to establish her in His will, plans, and purpose for her life. A true Woman of God knows that she is unable to be planted, grounded, or established outside of the headship and plan of God. Many women are wandering aimlessly trying to find some sort of purpose in the earth by aligning with many things, when it is their commitment that will establish them and cause them to walk into purpose.

Women who are committed to living inside of God have adapted the truth that apart from God they can do nothing. This takes away the unnecessary weight of perfectionism, comparison, and striving and allows the Godly woman to operate inside the power and ability of God. Too often, in order to accomplish God's plan, women feel the need to be super women when God always intended them to rely on Him.

John 15:5 I am the vine; you are the branches. If you remain in me and I in you, you will bear much fruit; apart from me you can do nothing.

As we live in a time and age where being an independent woman is seen as commendable and desirable, the Godly woman must know that, striving for strength in her own independence, is no match for the raw, authentic power that can only be drawn from dependence upon God. In modern culture, dependency is seen as a flaw and a deficiency. The kingdom woman knows that inside God's dependency is the only place that brings forth the fruit, fulfillment, and sustainability that she needs. John 15:5 is not negating the

55

fact that we, as women, are capable of much and are indeed strong in our abilities; however, it points to the truth that our identity comes from being an extension of God as we abide in Him and bear much fruit.

Outside of Christ, we may appear to be successful, strong, and fruitful, but our fruit will be lacking, limited, and void of God's fullness. This is the reason you see many women excelling in their businesses, ministries, relationships, and finances, yet still living an unfulfilled life. Anywhere you find a woman who is producing without God, you will likely find a woman who is empty and lacks purpose and fulfillment. God is the giver of life and He is the one who sustains that which He ordains.

Let's just pause and take a *Selah* pondering breath on that revelation for a moment.

The Godly woman is not only dependent upon Christ for her accomplishments or success, she relies on him for the essence of her very nature and identity. He creates the image in respect to how she should look, act, and present herself.

The Godly woman is identifiable by her resemblance and likeness to Christ.

MY GOD!

SHIFT!

Oftentimes, when looking at couples who have been joined in the covenant of marriage, I have observed that they eventually begin to act, think, and look like one another. The longer they are together, the easier it becomes to identify them as one. The woman of God should be so connected to Christ and the covenant she has built with Him that she begins to look like Him and begins to exude the essence of His glory, character, and nature.

Genesis 1:27 So God created human beings in his own likeness. He created them to be like himself. He created them as male and female.

It is in the DNA of the woman to embody the attributes and likeness of Christ. Although all of humankind has been made in the image of God, male and female, both have their own unique and innate character that reflects elements of the Father. The world has placed a major burden on womanhood, defining the woman's ability to marry, have children, and build a family. It is, however, important to note that Godly womanhood is indeed attainable in all phases and seasons of life whether or not these elements are present.

A Godly woman carries the ability to, not only to give birth naturally, but also to spiritually create, carry, birth, and nurture through Christ. Since she willingly commits and lays down her life, she is a natural receptor for the will of God, and for the things that He has strategically designed her to birth in the earth. Her identity is found in Christ and Christ alone. Remember, the Godly woman has the ability to operate in this identity solely because of her likeness to Christ and not because of her relationship status or her ability to carry what the world deems as worthiness and womanhood. If you have not yet come into alignment with your mate; if you are struggling to conceive, if you have not yet come into the fullness of God's promises for you, you are not any less a woman. The woman of God carries what God ordains her to carry and waits patiently and contently for the visions and promises of God to come to pass.

Habakkuk 2:3 For the vision is yet for an appointed time, but at the end it shall speak and not lie. Though it tarry, wait for it, because it will surely come; it will not tarry.

Let's just pause and take a *Selah* pondering breath on that revelation for a moment.

As God's women, we must choose to live in a place of contentment with what God has granted as our portion. Note that I used the word *choose* because God has allowed us to choose whether we will completely submit to His plan or to walk, kicking and screaming, through purpose. Your ability to excel in walking out your God-given purpose will be measured by your willingness to be disciplined and remain obedient before, during and after the hard seasons. This is not just a visual representation or facade that we present in society to appear godly; this is a life posture. The Woman of God is not merely concerned with presenting herself as Godly in physical form but lives that truth through the fear and reverence of the Lord.

Proverbs 31:30 Charm is deceitful, and beauty is vain, but a woman who fears the Lord is to be praised.

Many women in today's society have a heightened need to present themselves as flawless, beautiful, and appealing to those looking from the outside in. Some women in the body of Christ have slowly but surely found themselves assimilating with many of these standards in order to keep up with the times or in order to align with the culture. There has been an ungodly seek and desire for greater validation through the praise, accolades, and platforms, of this world.

Proverbs warns us of how empty and lifeless it is to find our worth in beauty alone. It teaches us that our strength and worth is not in our outward beauty, but in our fear and obedience unto the Lord. A kingdom woman does not fear rejection, her uniqueness, her lack of acceptance by the culture, or even those who proclaim to be in Christ. Her standards are built around her fear of the Lord and love for His law.

Many women find themselves lowering their standards, changing their expectations, or diminishing the modesty, holiness, and virtue that God is calling them to. As women of God, displeasing God must be greater than a fear of not being accepted by this world. Our inner beauty, built from our time with God, should display His nature and exude the fruit of the Spirit. This is the source of our modesty and our virtuous nature. It is the glory of the Lord that beautifies us and radiates us despite any adornment or outer workings.

1Peter 3:3-4 Your beauty should not come from outward adornment, such as elaborate hairstyles and the wearing of gold jewelry or fine clothes 4 but from the inner disposition of your heart, the unfading beauty of a gentle and quiet spirit, which is precious in God's sight.

Kingdom queens, it is time that we shed our tough exteriors and SHIFT out of hiding behind the makeup, designer clothing, and fine jewelry. There is nothing wrong with presenting yourself as royalty or taking pride in how you look, however, these areas should be additional adornments and not the source of your confidence and validation. God is looking for a woman whose heart is for Him.

- ✓ When he looks through all the outward things and into your heart, do you truly carry His nature and essence with confidence?

- ✓ Are you truly confident in the woman that He has called you to be and the mandate He has set for your life?

- ✓ Do you find joy in being set apart for His glory?

You do not have to boast, brag, or gloat regarding these standards in order to be seen by God. It is the positioning of your heart and a gentle spirit that are precious in God's sight.

Let's just pause and take a *Selah* pondering breath on that revelation for a moment.

When assessing "your" beauty standards and further aligning with "God'," ask yourself these questions:

- In what places have my standards for beauty become enmeshed with this world's?
- In what areas do I need to allow God to help me modestly embody Godly beauty?
- In what areas have I allowed this world to make me think that I can only be seen and received when I am boastful in my beauty?
- In what areas do I need healing in my confidence as a Woman of God?

Dictionary.com defines *characteristic* as "*a feature or quality belonging typically to a person, place, or thing and serving to identify it.*"

When we think about a Godly woman, everything she does, thinks, says, and embodies is from a posture of serving God and representing Him with her life. She is the standard of God in the earth and fulfills purpose through her very essence.

A Woman of God is essentially grounded, spiritually mature, disciplined, and confident in her ability to rest in God throughout every season. We will always be maturing to new levels and into deeper depths of becoming a Godly woman, but it is essential that we allow God to strip us of any and everything that keeps us from journeying with Him in these areas.

Deliverance Activation

1. What mindsets, regarding womanhood, need to be stripped from your identity that were not designed by God?
2. In what places have you submitted to the world's definition of what "Woman of God" means?
3. In order to greater embody biblical womanhood, what areas of your walk with Christ need more discipline?
4. To accept the truth that you are worthy of being a Godly woman, list the pains and disappointments where you need healing.
5. What do you like and dislike about being a Godly woman?

God wants to heal you and restore to you His original design and intent for womanhood. Know that you are fully seen, fully known, and fully loved by God. Whatever season you are in, God wants to bring restoration to you as a woman. God has a plan for you, even for the areas where you need healing in your identity as a woman.

Jeremiah 1:5 *I knew you before I formed you in your mother's womb. Before you were born, I set you apart and appointed you as my prophet to the nations.*

It is your time to arise and walk in what God has appointed for you as the Kingdom woman He has called you to be. He may be calling you to write a book, walk in covenant as a wife, break generational curses, lead your children, build a ministry, or launch your business. Wherever you are, there is grace for you inside of obedience. You do not have to be perfect to be a woman of God. You simply must be submitted. I pray that God aides you in the strength you need to fully submit to His plan for womanhood. No longer will you look to the world for validation or hope. May you find great joy in allowing the Holy Spirit to perfect you. I invite you to decree this declaration over yourself as you are journeying with God.

Decree Of The Godly Woman

"I declare that I am stepping into the full blueprint of who God ordained me to be as a Godly woman.

I declare that I am limitless, not in my own strength, but in my ability through God.

I declare that I lay my life down as a sacrifice daily and allow God to live, move, and create through me.

I declare that I will boast in my weaknesses and allow the strength of the Lord to rest upon me.

I declare that as I give myself permission to be imperfect, I am also consistently being perfected by God.

I declare that my beauty standards align with the heart of God and His thoughts towards me.

I declare that I am uniquely woven, I am Chosen, and I am enough.

I declare that as I am submitting to God; He is healing me and giving me the desires of my heart.

I declare that these declarations and decrees are established and aligned with who I am as God's chosen queen. It is so, in Jesu's name! Amen!

Characteristics Of A Godly Man

In the body of Christ, there tends to be more women's than men's ministries. Some men claim to be called to women, while men's ministries are scarce or centered more around activities rather than discipleship. Women tend to be ministered to more sufficiently on the following:

- ✓ Developing and cultivating their relationship with God
- ✓ Purifying themselves unto righteousness
- ✓ Keeping themselves holy
- ✓ Remaining virgins
- ✓ Consecrating and abstaining until marriage
- ✓ Focusing on God while single
- ✓ Preparing themselves personally, relationally, spiritually, financially to be a wife and for marriage

Men, however, do not seem to receive the same teaching and accountability. They are often left to decide these matters without sufficient discipleship and are often given the impression that they can have their pick of women, irrespective of personal responsibility or care for their hearts; there is no regard for purity, no intentionality to pursue relationship, and no desire to prepare for or consider marriage.

The number of men living for the Lord or attending church is significantly less as compared to women. There is also an increase in men being effeminate, homosexual, living on the down low, wanting to live as women (transgender), or not wanting to be married in the body of Christ or society as a whole. These factors play a role in the singleness of women and the reason there is a dominant number of consecrated women waiting to be married or resorting to living a fulfilled life of singleness.

Preparing men in the following areas needs to become a priority in the body of Christ:

- Have true covenant relationship with God
- Be godly men who understand their purpose, destiny, place in marriage, the family, and community
- Understand their role as leaders in marriage, family, and communities
- Honor and have godly relationships
- Regard the hearts, bodies, standards, and purposes of women
- Understand the purpose of godly marriage and want the covenant of marriage

When these areas are regarded, the following list of the characteristics of a godly man will not appear as far-fetched. Men and women will have better opportunities to explore relationships in a more comparable manner.

This list is intended to SHIFT you – the woman - to explore the qualities of a godly man beyond good looks, financial wealth, religious works, ministry endeavors, and spiritual gifts. Those qualities, though beneficial, are surface as compared to what is needed to build a solid foundation in a healthy relationship and a future godly marriage.

The man that comes into your life should possess the following attributes or at least demonstrate that he is working towards them. Remember, you should be able to demonstrate that you are working on what you are requiring of a boyfriend - potential mate. **These attributes are for him and for you.**

Covenant Relationship With God

He should want to be kept by God, have a strong covenant relationship with God, and be obedient to God, He should live through his covenant with God as a daily lifestyle.

He should be committed to hearing from God for himself and his future family so he can have vision for how to lead them in God's way and on God's path.

God should be the head of his life. He should love God more than anything else. Everything he does should flow through and out of his relationship with God.

John 17:3 And this is eternal life, that they may know You, the only true God, and Jesus Christ whom You have sent.

Romans 5:5-6 Now hope does not disappoint, because the love of God has been poured out in our hearts by the Holy Spirit who was given to us. For when we were still without strength, in due time Christ died for the ungodly.

Matthew 22:37 *Jesus said unto him, Thou shalt love the Lord thy God with all thy heart, and with all thy soul, and with all thy mind.*

John 14:15 *If you love Me, keep My commandments.*

John 14:17-18 *The Spirit of truth, whom the world cannot receive, because it neither sees Him nor knows Him; but you know Him, for He dwells with you and will be in you. I will not leave you orphans; I will come to you.*

Psalm 34:8-11 *Oh, taste and see that the LORD is good; Blessed is the man who trusts in Him! Oh, fear the LORD, you His saints! There is no want to those who fear Him. The young lions lack and suffer hunger; But those who seek the LORD shall not lack any good thing. Come, you children, listen to me; I will teach you the fear of the LORD.*

Isaiah 55:6 *Seek the LORD while He may be found, Call upon Him while He is near.*

Luke 11:9-13 *So I say to you, ask, and it will be given to you; seek, and you will find; knock, and it will be opened to you. For everyone who asks receives, and he who seeks finds, and to him who knocks it will be opened. If a son asks for bread from any father among you, will he give him a stone? Or if he asks for a fish, will he give him a serpent instead of a fish? Or if he asks for an egg, will he offer him a scorpion? If you then, being evil, know how to give good gifts to your children, how much more will your heavenly Father give the Holy Spirit to those who ask Him!*

John 4:23-24 *But the hour is coming, and now is, when the true worshipers will worship the Father in spirit and truth; for the Father is seeking such to worship Him. God is Spirit, and those who worship Him must worship in spirit and truth."*

John 8:31 *Then Jesus said to those Jews who believed Him, "If you abide in My word, you are My disciples indeed.*

John 15:5 *I am the vine, you are the branches. He who abides in Me, and I in him, bears much fruit; for without Me you can do nothing.*

John 15:14-17 *You are My friends if you do whatever I command you. No longer do I call you servants, for a servant does not know what his master is doing; but I have called you friends, for all things that I heard from My Father I have made known to you. You did not choose Me, but I chose you and appointed you that you should go and bear fruit, and that your fruit should remain, that whatever you ask the Father in My name He may give you. These things I command you, that you love one another.*

John 17:20-23 *I do not pray for these alone, but also for those who will believe in Me through their word; that they all may be one, as You, Father, are in Me, and I in You; that they also may be one in Us, that the world may believe that You sent Me. And the glory which You gave Me I have given them, that they may be one just as We are one: I in them, and You in Me; that they may be made perfect in one, and that the world may know that You have sent Me, and have loved them as You have loved Me.*

Matthew 6:33 Seek the Kingdom of God above all else, and live righteously, and he will give you everything you need.

Effective Prayer & Study Life

He should be demonstrating that he is a prayer warrior, have consistent communing with God, can hear and identify God's voice, is obedient to God and His word, possess good bible study habits and pursue or have a desire to be trained in his destiny and calling and who he is to be as an evolving man of God.

Provers 4:20-27 My son, attend to my words; incline thine ear unto my sayings. Let them not depart from thine eyes; keep them in the midst of thine heart. For they are life unto those that find them, and health to all their flesh. Keep thy heart with all diligence; for out of it are the issues of life. Put away from thee a froward mouth, and perverse lips put far from thee. Let thine eyes look right on, and let thine eyelids look straight before thee. Ponder the path of thy feet, and let all thy ways be established. Turn not to the right hand nor to the left: remove thy foot from evil.

James 4:5 Confess your faults one to another, and pray one for another, that ye may be healed. The effectual fervent prayer of a righteous man availeth much.

Mark 11:24 Therefore I tell you, whatever you ask for in prayer, believe that you have received it, and it will be yours.

Psalm 37:4 Take delight in the LORD, and he will give you the desires of your heart.

1John 5:14 This is the confidence we have in approaching God: that if we ask anything according to his will, he hears us.

2Timothy 2:15 Study to shew thyself approved unto God, a workman that needeth not to be ashamed, rightly dividing the word of truth.

Luke 21:3 Watch therefore, and pray always that you may be counted worthy to escape all these things that will come to pass, and to stand before the Son of Man.

2Peter 3:18 Rather, you must grow in the grace and knowledge of our Lord and Savior Jesus Christ. All glory to him, both now and forever! Amen.

Destiny Pursuit

He should have a sense of clarify regarding his purpose in life and be working towards bringing it to pass.

Proverbs 16:9 A man's heart deviseth his way: but the Lord directeth his steps.

Philippians 1:6 And I am sure of this, that he who began a good work in you will bring it to completion at the day of Jesus Christ.

Psalm 138:8 The Lord will fulfill his purpose for me; your steadfast love, O Lord, endures forever. Do not forsake the work of your hands.

Healthy Identity/Sonship

He should have a healthy God identity or should at least be working towards possessing a good sense of self and who he is in God.

**Genesis 1:26-27** And God said, Let us make man in our image, after our likeness: and let them have dominion over the fish of the sea, and over the fowl of the air, and over the cattle, and over all the earth, and over every creeping thing that creepeth upon the earth.

**Psalm 139:14** I will praise thee; for I am fearfully and wonderfully made: marvellous are thy works; and that my soul knoweth right well.

**Psalm 139:17** How precious also are thy thoughts unto me, O God! how great is the sum of them!

**Psalm 40:5** Many, O LORD my God, are the wonders You have done, and the plans You have for us--none can compare to You--if I proclaim and declare them, they are more than I can count.

**Jeremiah 29:11** For I know the thoughts that I think toward you, saith the LORD, thoughts of peace, and not of evil, to give you an expected end.

**Ephesians 2:10** For we are God's masterpiece, created to do good works which God prepared in advance for us to do.

**Ephesians 4:24** And to put on the new self, created after the likeness of God in true righteousness and holiness.

1Peter 2:9 But you are a chosen generation, a royal priesthood, a holy nation, His own special people, that you may proclaim the praises of Him who called you out of darkness into His marvelous light.

Ephesians 1:4-5 Just as He chose us in Him before the foundation of the world, that we should be holy and without blame before Him in love, having predestined us to adoption as sons by Jesus Christ to Himself, according to the good pleasure of His will.

John 3:16 For God so loved the world, that he gave his only Son, that whoever believes in him should not perish but have eternal life.

Galatians 3:26 For in Christ Jesus you are all sons of God, through faith.

2Corinthians 5:17 Therefore, if anyone is in Christ, he is a new creation. The old has passed away; behold, the new has come.

1Peter 2:9 But you are a chosen race, a royal priesthood, a holy nation, a people for his own possession, that you may proclaim the excellencies of him who called you out of darkness into his marvelous light.

Galatians 2:20 I have been crucified with Christ. It is no longer I who live, but Christ who lives in me. And the life I now live in the flesh I live by faith in the Son of God, who loved me and gave himself for me.

John 15:15 No longer do I call you servants, for the servant does not know what his master is doing; but I have

75

*called you friends, for all that I have heard from my Father
I have made known to you.*

*John 1:12 But to all who did receive him, who believed in
his name, he gave the right to become children of God.*

*Romans 8:17 And if children, then heirs—heirs of God and
fellow heirs with Christ, provided we suffer with him in
order that we may also be glorified with him.*

Healed Of Trauma

He should be healed of pass relationship traumas or at least
be healthy enough in his manhood to work through them as
they surface in his interactions with you. He should not be
having you pay for what other women did to him.

He should be able to process through mother issues and
already have some wellness and balance in this area where
he is not trying to make you fulfill mother issues. He
should be at the place where he can leave and cleave
properly such that family members are put into proper
perspective as he grows in relationship with you.

He should be able to process through father issues and
already possess some wellness this area. He should want to
be a good father and covering for his family. As you all
evolve in relationship, his character should be
demonstrating that of a responsible and accountable
protector, provider, visionary, and covering. He should be
displaying a love for God, love for himself, his future wife,
and children.

3John 2:2 Beloved, I wish above all things that thou mayest prosper and be in health, even as thy soul prospereth.

Breaking Generational Curses

He should have a mindset and pursuit of breaking generational strongholds, curses, and nullifying and overthrowing every demon, curse, vow, and covenant that hinders the blessings of God from flowing in his life, his family line, the relationship, and his future generations.

Ephesians 6:12 For we wrestle not against flesh and blood, but against principalities, against powers, against the rulers of the darkness of this world, against spiritual wickedness in high places.

Matthew 16:19 And I will give unto thee the keys of the kingdom of heaven: and whatsoever thou shalt bind on earth shall be bound in heaven: and whatsoever thou shalt loose on earth shall be loosed in heaven.

James 4:7 Submit yourselves, then, to God. Resist the devil, and he will flee from you.

John 10:10 The thief comes only to steal and kill and destroy; I have come that they may have life, and have it to the full."

Colossians 1:13-14 For he has rescued us from the dominion of darkness and brought us into the kingdom of the Son he loves, in whom we have redemption, the forgiveness of sins.

John 16:33 I [Jesus] have told you these things, so that in me you may have peace. In this world you will have trouble. But take heart! I have overcome the world.

1Corinthians 10:13 No temptation has overtaken you except what is common to mankind. And God is faithful; he will not let you be tempted beyond what you can bear. But when you are tempted, he will also provide a way out so that you can endure it.

Galatians 3:13 Christ hath redeemed us from the curse of the law, being made a curse for us: for it is written, Cursed is every one that hangeth on a tree.

Exodus 20:5 Thou shalt not bow down thyself to them, nor serve them: for I the LORD thy God am a jealous God, visiting the iniquity of the fathers upon the children unto the third and fourth generation of them that hate me.

Ezekiel 18:19-20 Yet say ye, Why? doth not the son bear the iniquity of the father? When the son hath done that which is lawful and right, and hath kept all my statutes, and hath done them, he shall surely live.

Numbers 14:18 The LORD is longsuffering, and of great mercy, forgiving iniquity and transgression, and by no means clearing the guilty, visiting the iniquity of the fathers upon the children unto the third and fourth generation.

Repented Heart

He should possess godly sorrow for sin, a repentant heart, being quick in turning back to God for restoration.

1 John 1:9 If we confess our sins, he is faithful and just and will forgive us our sins and purify us from all unrighteousness.

Acts 3:19 Repent, then, and turn to God, so that your sins may be wiped out, that times of refreshing may come from the Lord.

Mathew 3:8 Produce fruit in keeping with repentance.

Fear of The Lord

He should have a healthy reverence for the Lord and understand the need, power, protection, and safety of loving, honoring, and fearing God.

Proverbs 1:7 The fear of the LORD is the beginning of knowledge: but fools despise wisdom and instruction.

Proverbs 8:13 The fear of the LORD is to hate evil: pride, and arrogancy, and the evil way, and the froward mouth, do I hate.

Psalm 33:8 Let all the earth fear the LORD: let all the inhabitants of the world stand in awe of him.

Proverbs 14:27 The fear of the LORD is a fountain of life, to depart from the snares of death.

Proverbs 14:26 In the fear of the LORD is strong confidence: and his children shall have a place of refuge.

Psalm 25:14 The secret of the LORD is with them that fear him; and he will shew them his covenant.

Proverbs 3:7 Be not wise in thine own eyes: fear the LORD, and depart from evil.

Psalm 86:11 Teach me thy way, O LORD; I will walk in thy truth: unite my heart to fear thy name.

Luke 1:50 And his mercy is on them that fear him from generation to generation.

Psalms 34:9 O fear the LORD, ye his saints: for there is no want to them that fear him.

Humility & Self-Sacrificing

He should be humble, compassionate, concerned about your well-being and self-sacrificing for the sake of what pleases and honors God, you, the relationship, and your future together.

He should be willing to humble himself and live in a posture of humility and meekness before God. He should be willing to cast himself down so God can be exalted in him, and though he possesses self-confidence, he is not puffed up in his identity, manhood, abilities, and accomplishments. In his posture as a laid-down lover before God, he is able to love you as God loves you - as God loves the church.

Ephesians 5:25 Husbands, love your wives, even as Christ also loved the church, and gave himself for it.

Philippians 2:3-4 Do nothing out of selfish ambition or vain conceit. Rather, in humility value others above yourselves, not looking to your own interests but each of you to the interests of the others.

Forgiving
He should be forgiving and willing to move forward, releasing grace and setting healthy goals that extinguish being resentful, vengeful, or begrudging.

Ephesians 4:32 Be kind and compassionate to one another, forgiving each other, just as in Christ God forgave you.

Responsible & Accountable
He should reject making excuses for falling into temptation, being irresponsible in life, or for how he governs your heart. He should have a fear of the Lord and should want to be kept by God's principles through the power of the Holy Spirit.

Romans 14:12 So then, each of us will give an account of ourselves to God.

1Peter 1:4-5 To an inheritance incorruptible, and undefiled, and that fadeth not away, reserved in heaven for you, Who are kept by the power of God through faith unto salvation ready to be revealed in the last time.

Truthful & Honest
He should be honest and trustworthy. You should be able to trust him to speak truth and want truth. He should be able to speak his truth, discern when his truth may not be godly, healthy, or beneficial even it if is how he feels or

believes. Simultaneously, he should be able to receive and apply the truth of God to his situations.

Proverbs 12:22 The Lord detests lying lips but delights in people who are trustworthy.

Wisdom
He should seek the wisdom of the Lord so that he can possess revelation, knowledge, strategy, counsel, and witty ideas to resolve issues, make healthy decisions, and lead in a responsible and godly manner.

Proverbs 3:13 Blessed are those who find wisdom, those who gain understanding.

Generous
He should be generous and have a heart to bless you, There is reaping and sowing into the good ground of who you are in life, who you are to him, and who you are to God.

2Corinthians 9:6 Remember this: Whoever sows sparingly will also reap sparingly, and whoever sows generously will also reap generously.

Standards For A Godly Mate
He should have a standard of what qualities his wife should have. He should possess some revelation regarding the reason these standards are important to his life and who he is as he evolves in destiny.

Proverbs 12:4 *A wife of noble character is her husband's crown, but a disgraceful wife is like decay in his bones.*

Proverbs 18:22 *He who finds a wife finds a good thing, And obtains favor from the LORD.*

Proverbs 19:14 *Houses and wealth are inherited from parents, but a prudent wife is from the LORD.*

Proverbs 5:18–19 *May your fountain be blessed, and may you rejoice in the wife of your youth. A loving doe, a graceful deer— may her breasts satisfy you always, may you ever be intoxicated with her love.*

Isaiah 34:16 *Seek and read from the book of the Lord: Not one of these shall be missing; none shall be without her mate. For the mouth of the Lord has commanded, and his Spirit has gathered them.*

Genesis 24:1-4 *Abraham was now very old, and the Lord had blessed him in every way. He said to the senior servant in his household, the one in charge of all that he had, "Put your hand under my thigh. I want you to swear by the Lord, the God of heaven and the God of earth, that you will not get a wife for my son from the daughters of the Canaanites, among whom I am living, but will go to my country and my own relatives and get a wife for my son Isaac.*

Lifestyle of Holiness

He should desire holiness and not want to stumble into or draw you into distraction, sin, or behaviors that cause you to do or become less than what God is requiring of you.

1Peter 1:16 Because it is written, Be ye holy; for I am holy.

Leviticus 11:44 For I am the Lord your God: ye shall therefore sanctify yourselves, and ye shall be holy; for I am holy: neither shall ye defile yourselves with any manner of creeping thing that creepeth upon the earth.

Regard For Righteous Boundaries

He should be striving to be delivered from perversions and lusts and not hold on to perverse mindsets and behaviors that he might unleash in the marriage.

If he does not honor you in dating, respect your boundaries, or view your body as sacred and pure, he will not honor you in marriage. Many women allow men to talk them into engaging in sexual acts that he claims is not sinning because there is no penetration; yet, God says otherwise. This is manipulation of you, the flesh, and the Word of God. This is a red flag to how things will be in the marriage. Many married women end up being sexual slaves, raped in marriage, and sexually unfulfilled, because their husbands had no regard for who they are as an intimate covenant partner. He was only interested in what she could do for him sexually so he can release. Please understand that anytime you are forced to do something you do not want to do, and you say "no," or whether in dating or in marriage, and he does it anyway, that is rape. This may be alarming or even triggering but it is important that we, as women, gain clarity into what the boundary line is in this area so men will stop crossing it. Religion and freaky undelivered saints teach us that everything goes in the marriage bed, and abusive acts are approved by God. but undefiled does not mean perverse.

What you deem fun, liberating, and needful, could be an abomination in the eyes of God, even within the confines of marriage. This is the reason it is so important to be restored unto holiness rather than holding on to perverse ways and mindsets.

Allowing God to purify you in holiness, will SHIFT you into truth and clarity regarding what is appropriate in the marriage bed and what the boundary lines are for you and your spouse. There are some lines that cannot be crossed because it may open a door to past sins, generational bondage, or greater bondages of perversions. Only being restored in holiness will SHIFT you to wanting to know truths about yourself and your spouse, and how to honor God, each other, and your marriage bed.

Hebrews 13:4 Marriage should be honored by all, and the marriage bed kept pure, for God will judge the adulterer and all the sexually immoral.

Proverbs 31:3 Give not thy strength unto women, nor thy ways to that which destroyeth kings.

1Corinthians 6:19-20 Or do you not know that your body is a temple of the Holy Spirit within you, whom you have from God? You are not your own, for you were bought with a price. So glorify God in your body.

Romans 12:1-3 I beseech you therefore, brethren, by the mercies of God, that you present your bodies a living sacrifice, holy, acceptable to God, which is your reasonable service. And do not be conformed to this world, but be transformed by the renewing of your mind, that you may prove what is that good and acceptable and perfect will of God. For I say, through the grace given to me, to everyone who is among you, not to think of himself more highly than he ought to think, but to think soberly, as God has dealt to each one a measure of faith.

Effective Communicator

Communication is the greatest form of intimacy. If you cannot communicate outside of bedroom, you surely will not communicate in the bedroom. If you do not communicate in dating, you will struggle with communicating and building a strong healthy marriage. If you do not learn effective tools that help you identify, process, explore, and express your thoughts and feelings in a healthy way, you are doing yourself, God, and those who are in a relationship a disservice. You cannot adequately represent the character and nature of God without knowing how to properly manage and express yourself. When your thoughts, feelings, and voice are silent, shutdown, distorted, or toxic, you force others to try and figure out what you are thinking, feeling, needing, and desiring. Blaming our parents and childhood for not teaching you how to express yourself is a juvenile excuse. If you are 18 years of age or older, the responsibility just SHIFTED to you. This is part of ADULTING. If you want to remain a juvenile and silent in your emotions, do not get married.

Giving men passes for not being communicators is not godly and is unbiblical. God is clear about what He thinks, how He feels, what He desires, what He needs, and what He desires. We are all created in His image. Communication is not sexist or gender biases. It is innate and critical to our living in emotional, physical, and spiritual wellness as a lifestyle. Every ADULT should learn heathy emotional, interpersonal, social, communication, anger management, and conflict resolution skills. It is a flag when a man is not willing to learn how to steward his emotional wellness in a healthy manner. Stop giving your heart, time, and emotions, to men who will break your heart because they reject growing into maturity as an ADULT. In counseling over twenty years and counting, I hate to acknowledge the countless times I have hear married women say:

- I cannot talk to him
- He will not communicate with me
- He does not express his thoughts and feelings
- He does not listen to me
- He holds everything inside
- I only know how he feels or thinks when he wants sex

I wish I could say this is mostly non-Christian men. But the truth is, it is mostly Christian men. The women will go on and on making excuses for the reason the man is like this. Yet they are miserable, voiceless, left in the dark, and often succumb to witchcraft tactics to try and figure out what their husband needs and wants. Part of this is the fault of the body of Christ. Leaders make excuses for the reason men do not communicate. These excuses are often bias, sexist, and worldly. There is minimal effort to teach men emotional wellness. And therefore, we have a church full of macho, prideful, noncommunicating men who claim to lead us and our families. Yet we have no clue where they are going, what God is saying, how they are doing, and whether they will stay the course of their journey. We are being blindly led by silent men who think we should just trust them. They are not God. God does not require us to blindly trust anyone. It is a false narrative that leads to broken hearts, broken ministries, broken generations.

Women, if the man cannot communicate or does not want to learn, do not marry him. Do not enter a marriage where you have to be a psychic, a witch, or have to constantly pray and be Inspector Gadget to figure out a man.

Proverbs 13:17 An unreliable messenger stumbles into trouble, but a reliable messenger brings healing.

Proverbs 18:21 The tongue can bring death or life; those who love to talk will reap the consequences.

Proverbs 18:13 Spouting off before listening to the facts is both shameful and foolish.

Colossians 4:6 Let your conversation be gracious and attractive[a] so that you will have the right response for everyone.

Proverbs 25:11 The Amplified Bible A word fitly spoken and in due season is like apples of gold in settings of silver.

Proverbs 15:28 The heart of the godly thinks carefully before speaking; the mouth of the wicked overflows with evil words.

Matthew 5: 23-24 Therefore, if you are offering your gift at the altar and there remember that your brother or sister has something against you, 24 leave your gift there in front of the altar. First go and be reconciled to them; then come and offer your gift.

Proverbs 15:7 The lips of the wise disperse knowledge, But the heart of the fool does not do so.

Marriage Preparation

If he says he is desiring to be married, he should be seeking God for revelation of what it means to be a godly married man and seeking to acquire those attributes in his life. He should be seeking to have a steady job, consistent career, fixing his credit or already have good credit. He should have a mindset for investing or generating wealth and legacy. He should be independent in his mobility such that he has a car or is able to get where he needs to go sufficiently; he should have his own apartment or home, be a decent housekeeper or able to pay for housekeeping services, eager to upkeep the home by making sure things get fixed and work properly. These areas are important because the man cannot be in love with the idea of marriage. He must position himself for the reality of marriage. Sometimes the meeting of a good woman will spark this in a man. Make sure you see and experience his change of responsibility and caretaking in this area. Make sure he is not feeding you fluff regarding marriage but is not adequately positioning himself to be the reality of a husband in your life and to the future family you will build.

Genesis 2:15 Then the Lord God took the man and put him in the garden of Eden to tend and keep it.

Genesis 2:22-24 And the rib, which the Lord God had taken from man, made he a woman, and brought her unto the man. And Adam said, This is now bone of my bones, and flesh of my flesh: she shall be called Woman, because she was taken out of Man. Therefore shall a man leave his father and his mother, and shall cleave unto his wife: and they shall be one flesh.

1Timothy 5:8 *But if anyone does not provide for his own, and especially for those of his household, he has denied the faith and is worse than an unbeliever.*

Ephesians 5:22-33 *Wives, be subject to your own husbands, as to the Lord. For the husband is the head of the wife, as Christ also is the head of the church, He Himself being the Savior of the body. But as the church is subject to Christ, so also the wives ought to be to their husbands in everything. Husbands, love your wives, just as Christ also loved the church and gave Himself up for her, so that He might sanctify her, having cleansed her by the washing of water with the word, that He might present to Himself the church in all her glory, having no spot or wrinkle or any such thing; but that she would be holy and blameless. So husbands ought also to love their own wives as their own bodies. He who loves his own wife loves himself; for no one ever hated his own flesh, but nourishes and cherishes it, just as Christ also does the church, because we are members of His body. For this reason a man shall leave his father and mother and shall be joined to his wife, and the two shall become one flesh. This mystery is great; but I am speaking with reference to Christ and the church. Nevertheless, each individual among you also is to love his own wife even as himself, and the wife must see to it that she respects her husband.*

Help Mate Qualities

Though it is healthy to support and be a blessing at times, do not start engaging in wifely duties of cooking, cleaning, shacking, sexing, driving the man around in your car, as this dependence becomes set in your foundation. Be clear about what you desire in a husband as it relates to domestic duties and assistance, so you will not become his maid in the marriage. Especially if you are a career woman, a business owner, or operate in consistent ministry. Do not take on full domestic duties that you are not able to keep up with, or that you will dread doing later because you have given the impression that you will be Wonder Woman to this man and to the home.

Genesis 2:18 And the Lord God said, It is not good that the man should be alone; I will make him an help meet for him.

1Peter 3:7 Likewise, ye husbands, dwell with them according to knowledge, giving honour unto the wife, as unto the weaker vessel, and as being heirs together of the grace of life; that your prayers be not hindered.

1Corinthians 11:3 I want you to realize that the head of every man is Christ, and the head of the woman is man, and the head of Christ is God.

Colossians 3: 18-19 Wives, submit yourselves to your husbands, as is fitting in the Lord. Husbands, love your wives and do not be harsh with them.

Enduring & Persevering
He should possess the quality to persevere, lead in hard times, and allow you to be a support as he seeks to persevere and lead in hard seasons.

James 1:12 Blessed is the one who perseveres under trial because, having stood the test, that person will receive the crown of life that the Lord has promised to those who love him.

John 10:28-30 I give them eternal life, and they shall never perish; no one will snatch them out of my hand. My Father, who has given them to me, is greater than all; no one can snatch them out of my Father's hand. I and the Father are one.

Jude 1:24-25 To him who is able to keep you from stumbling and to present you before his glorious presence without fault and with great joy to the only God our Savior be glory, majesty, power and authority, through Jesus Christ our Lord, before all ages, now and forevermore! Amen.

Romans 8:37-39 No, in all these things we are more than conquerors through him who loved us. For I am convinced that neither death nor life, neither angels nor demons, neither the present nor the future, nor any powers, neither height nor depth, nor anything else in all creation, will be able to separate us from the love of God that is in Christ Jesus our Lord.

Eternal Learner

He should be teachable and ever learning. He should want to make you better, make himself better, and to be better as he advances in life. He should not be comfortable with being stagnant in his identity, walk with God, or success in life. He should endeavor to evolve in destiny as a lifestyle with Jesus Christ. He should be open to rebuke, chastisement, and constructive criticism so he can be transformed and continuously growing in the maturity of the Lord.

Psalm 1:1-3 Blessed is the man who walks not in the counsel of the ungodly, nor stands in the path of sinners, nor sits in the seat of the scornful; But his delight is in the law of the Lord, and in His law he meditates day and night. He shall be like a tree planted by the rivers of water, that brings forth its fruit in its season, whose leaf also shall not wither; and whatever he does shall prosper.

Proverbs 12:1 Whoso loveth instruction loveth knowledge: but he that hateth reproof is brutish.

Proverbs 9:9 Give instruction to a wise man, and he will be yet wiser: teach a just man, and he will increase in learning.

Proverbs 4:5 Get wisdom, get understanding: forget it not; neither decline from the words of my mouth.

2Timothy 3:16 All scripture is given by inspiration of God, and is profitable for doctrine, for reproof, for correction, for instruction in righteousness:

Hebrews 12:6 For whom the Lord loveth he chasteneth, and scourgeth every son whom he receiveth.

Brave
He should be brave, courageous, and God fearing in the face of obstacles and adversity. He should have an

understanding that God is with you and will SHIFT him to successful victory.

Deuteronomy 31:6 *Be strong and courageous. Do not be afraid or terrified because of them, for the Lord your God goes with you; he will never leave you nor forsake you.*

Psalms 118:6 *The Lord is on my side; I will not fear. What can man do to me?*

Isaiah 41:10 *Fear thou not; for I am with thee: be not dismayed; for I am thy God: I will strengthen thee; yea, I will help thee; yea, I will uphold thee with the right hand of my righteousness.*

Isaiah 40:31 *But those who hope in the Lord will renew their strength. They will soar on the wings like eagles; they will run and not grow weary, they will walk and not be faint."*

Isaiah 54:17 *No weapon that is formed against thee shall prosper; and every tongue that shall rise against thee in judgment thou shalt condemn. This is the heritage of the servants of the LORD, and their righteousness is of me, saith the LORD.*

1Corinthians 16:13 *Watch, stand fast in the faith, be brave, be strong.*

Romans 8:28 *And we know that all things work together for good to those who love God, to those who are the called according to His purpose.*

Philippians 4:19 And my God shall supply all your need according to His riches in glory by Christ Jesus.

Deliverance Activation

1. Journal your thoughts on the attributes above.

2. Ask God for his standard for your and for your godly mate and the purpose to which he is to have these standards.

3. Ask God for revelation on the standards you are to have to be equally yoked with your mate.

4. Ask God to give you three to five goals to work on to prepare for dating; to prepare for marriage.

5. As you would date, share this chapter with him; work together to set goals to SHIFT together in greater character and fortification as a godly person and as a godly couple.

Birthing Holiness In A Believer

In this day and age, when sin is addressed, a person will say *"You are judging me. Christians are so judgmental."* Yet God's nature and character is righteousness. His very essence is holiness.

Isaiah 6:3 *And one cried unto another, and said, Holy, holy, holy, is the LORD of hosts: the whole earth is full of his glory.*

Revelations 4:8 *And the four beasts had each of them six wings about him; and they were full of eyes within: and they rest not day and night, saying, Holy, holy, holy, Lord God Almighty, which was, and is, and is to come.*

The holiness of God is undeniable. Holiness is who he is. Holiness is foundational for living in covenant with him, worshipping him, reverencing him. We cannot deny his holiness yet claim he is our God.

We should be a knowing the truth of God's holiness and keeping one another accountable to being holy. Unholiness separates us from God's truth, protection, and the right standing of representing and living in and for him.

We can act like sin is ok or dilute God's nature with our perception, but it does not change the fact that God is holy, the entire standard of living in him is to be holy. He desires us to pursue and be holy.

1Peter 1:16 *Because it is written, Be ye holy; for I am holy.*

Leviticus 11:44 For I am the Lord your God: ye shall therefore sanctify yourselves, and ye shall be holy; for I am holy: neither shall ye defile yourselves with any manner of creeping thing that creepeth upon the earth.

Hebrews 12:14 *Make every effort to live in peace with everyone and to be holy; without holiness no one will see the Lord.*

1Corinthians 1:2 *To the church of God in Corinth, to those sanctified in Christ Jesus and called to be his holy people, together with all those everywhere who call on the name of our Lord Jesus Christ—their Lord and ours.*

<u>*Holy*</u> means to be:
1. viewed as a saint of God
2. be set apart
3. deemed sacred (physically, pure, morally blameless or religious, ceremonially, consecrated)

When we reject holiness and the need to pursue holiness, our perception about God becomes a false reality. Such deception will have us serving a false god that we created in our own thinking, rather than the true and living holy God.

1Peter 1:13-17 The Message Bible *So roll up your sleeves, put your mind in gear, be totally ready to receive the gift that's coming when Jesus arrives. Don't lazily slip back into those old grooves of evil, doing just what you feel like doing. You didn't know any better then; you do now. As obedient children, let yourselves be pulled into a way of life shaped by God's life, a life energetic and blazing with holiness. God said, "I am holy; you be holy." You call out*

97

to God for help and he helps—he's a good Father that way. But don't forget, he's also a responsible Father, and won't let you get by with sloppy living. Your life is a journey you must travel with a deep consciousness of God.

King James Bible *Wherefore gird up the loins of your mind, be sober, and hope to the end for the grace that is to be brought unto you at the revelation of Jesus Christ; As obedient children, not fashioning yourselves according to the former lusts in your ignorance: But as he which hath called you is holy, so be ye holy in all manner of conversation; Because it is written, Be ye holy; for I am holy. And if ye call on the Father, who without respect of persons judgeth according to every man's work, pass the time of your sojourning here in fear.*

Conversation is _anastrophē_ in Greek and means:
1. manner of life, conduct
2. behavior, conversation, deportment
3. demeanor; conduct; behavior, the conduct or obedience of a child in school - basically act like a child of God - not just in talk but in action and lifestyle

It is interesting that scripture uses the word, "conversation," which would give the impression that it is defining the speaking of words, but conversation means your conduct, behavior and way of life. I asked God the reason for that and He said, "What you speak should be what you live and what comes out of you is what you live. If you claim to live holy but your conduct and lifestyle is not holy, then your conversation is demonstrating that you live a lie and are a liar."

James1:22 But be ye doers of the word, and not hearers only, deceiving your own selves.

Deceiving is *paralogizomai* in the Greek and means:
1. to misreckon, i.e. delude
2. beguile (to influence by trickery, flattery, cheat, divert, charm, basically bewitch)
3. deceive, to reckon wrong, miscount, to cheat by false reckoning, to deceive by false reasoning, circumvent (to avoid (defeat, failure, unpleasantness, etc.) by artfulness or deception; avoid by anticipating or outwitting)

When you are not adorned in the word, you are bewitching yourself by trying to charm and mislead others into believing a lie about you.

Holiness is a heart posture, not a religious posture.

Luke 6:45 A good man brings good things out of the good stored up in his heart, and an evil man brings evil things out of the evil stored up in his heart. For the mouth speaks what the heart is full of.

Matthew 15:18 But those things which proceed out of the mouth come forth from the heart; and they defile the man.

Your heart must love the things that God loves and hate the things that God hates. You must also love and hate them in spite of the pleasures you may receive from them or how others may feel or believe regarding them.

Psalm 97:10 Ye that love the LORD, hate evil: he preserveth the souls of his saints; he delivereth them out of the hand of the wicked.

Psalm 51:10 Create in me a clean heart, O God; and renew a right spirit within me.

This scripture demonstrates a posture of submission to God working His holiness in you. It is also a yearning to be like God. It is a cry to be clean, righteous, holy and pure. It is a pursuit to be exactly as God desires you to be - not like you want to be, but how God wants you to be.

Our heart pursues, chooses, and manifests holiness.

Create is *bârâ'* in Hebrew and means:
1. (absolutely) to create; (qualified) to cut down (a wood)
2. select, feed (as formative processes)
3. choose, create (creator), dispatch, do, make (fat), to form, shape, transform
4. to be created of heaven and earth, of birth, of something new, of miracles

Clean is *tahor* in the Hebrew and means:
1. pure (in a physical, chemical, ceremonial or moral sense)
2. clean, fair, pure(-ness), morally and ethically pure

Psalm 24:4 He who has clean hands and a pure heart, who does not lift up his soul to falsehood, who does not swear deceitfully.

Ezekiel 18:31 Cast away from yourselves all the transgressions you have committed, and fashion for yourselves a new heart and a new spirit. Why should you die, O house of Israel?

Ezekiel 36:26 *I will give you a new heart and put a new spirit within you; I will remove your heart of stone and give you a heart of flesh.*

Ephesians 2:20 *For we are his workmanship, created in Christ Jesus unto good works, which God hath before ordained that we should walk in them.*

Galatians 6:15 *For in Christ Jesus neither circumcision availeth any thing, nor uncircumcision, but a new creature.*

Ephesians 4:24 *and to put on the new self, created to be like God in true righteousness and holiness.*

Colossians 3:10 *and have put on the new self, which is being renewed in knowledge in the image of its Creator.*

2Timothy 2:21 *So if anyone cleanses himself of what is unfit, he will be a vessel for honor: sanctified, useful to the Master, and prepared for every good work.*

Titus 2:14 *He gave Himself for us to redeem us from all lawlessness and to purify for Himself a people for His own possession, zealous for good deeds.*

When you pursue holiness, you are asking for God and His standards to be fashioned in you. One of the words for 'clean' is 'miracles,' so this birthing is miraculous - miraculously invading your life with heaven, miraculously birthing holiness like God would birth a child in you or a vision.

Another reason people reject holiness is because they have a wrong spirit within them. David had to ask for a right spirit to be put in him.

Psalms 51:10 Create in me a clean heart, O God; and renew a right spirit within me.

Renew means *"to be new, renew, repair, to be rebuild."*

It is only a wrong spirit, one that is not God's spirit, that would not want to be holy or that would think you are religious for judging their lack of holiness when God is holy and wants us to be holy like He is holy.

You must fall out of agreement with the wrong spirit operating in you. You must pursue a clean heart and desire the restoration of God's right spirit in you.

Proverbs 6:16-19 New International Bible There are six things the Lord hates, seven that are detestable to him: haughty eyes, a lying tongue, hands that shed innocent blood, a heart that devises wicked schemes, feet that are quick to rush into evil, a false witness who pours out lies and a person who stirs up conflict in the community.

Holiness is God. Holiness is a defense - a shield. It is a guard for the upright. It secures our salvation while protecting us from evil and ungodliness.

Psalm 7:10 My defense is of God, which saveth the upright in heart.
New International Bible My shield is with God, who saves the upright in heart.

Psalm 7:9-10 *Oh, let the wickedness of the wicked come to an end, but establish the [uncompromisingly] righteous [those upright and in harmony with You]; for You, Who try the hearts and emotions and thinking powers, are a righteous God. My defense and shield depend on God, Who saves the upright in heart.*

Matthew 5:8 *Blessed are the pure in heart, for they will see God.*

<-->

How Do You Know Holiness Is Birthed In You?

1. When God is the head of your life and you only want what God wants for you.

2. When the Holy Spirit is the guide of your life and you are convicted by even the smallest of sins or even the thought of sin.

3. When thoughts and acts of sin have you crying out to be cleansed and renewed in God's holiness.

4. When you are appalled with things defiling your heart and life, even subtle things or things that come in unaware.

5. When you live guarding your heart and life because you do not want to be defiled.

6. When you are appalled at people who try to get you to lower your standards of holiness and when you will sacrifice pleasures, opportunities, and relationships to remain holy.

7. When you want to please God with all your heart, and it grieves you to displease him.

8. When you are easily repentant even if you are justified in behaving ungodly, offended, or vengeful.

9. When you know your victory is in pleasing God, not winning against, controlling, or overpowering other people or situations.

10. When you care about how your actions represent God - whether you have and live through His character and nature.

11. When you care about how your actions impact people and situations.

12. When you are not trying to sneak and sin and get your needs and desires met.

13. When you no longer boast in sin or glory in the fact that you got away with it; sinning people boast within themselves - in their thoughts or hearts; they are proud that they sinned or got away with it, or they brag to others about it - giving the appearance that it is okay to sin. This is pride - it is self-glory. Pride and idolatry come before the fall - Proverbs 16:18.

14. When you CHOOSE not to say it or do it even though you want to sooooooo badly.

15. When you do not make excuses for unholiness or abuse God's grace.

16. When you do not defile or defame God by making Him unholy in order to justify your unholiness.

17. When you seek support to keep you from sinning rather than secretly struggling as this slowly yields you to sin. Willpower is your own strength working. Willpower will not keep you. It just tricks you into believing you are delivered and free, at least until it gives out on you again. Imaginations and desires eventually outlive willpower. Willpower keeps reminding you of your sin by counting the days that you withheld, when you should be so free that you start to forget you were ever bound. You need support systems and accountability partners who care about living holy and who care about your living holy - who will help provide keys to living through the Holy Spirit so you can be free and holy.

18. When you do not become offended because your unholiness is called out or is being exposed - you embrace accountability and correction over your sin.

19. When you do not try to cover or lie your way out of sin when you are called out or exposed - you accept accountability and pursue change.

20. When you can forsake platform, fame, fortune, validation, your reputation (saving face) for holiness.

21. When you become your own accountability partner where you do not wait to be exposed or convicted, your

own inner man quickens you to the caution of yielding to sin.

22. When your virtue and purity is part of your lifestyle where you care about how you physically look, what you wear, how you treat and present your body and making sure it does not draw away from God, defame God, or dull your witness of God. *1Corinthians 6:19 What? know ye not that your body is the temple of the Holy Ghost which is in you, which ye have of God, and ye are not your own?*

23. When your virtue and purity is part of your lifestyle where you care about how you physically look, what you wear, how you treat and present your body and making sure God is pleased with you - what others do, eat, wear, you may not be able to do. God's standard for your appearance may be different from someone else; will you be okay with His unique identity in and upon you?

24. When there is no plain B, especially where worldly or demonic plans are options to fulfilling your needs and desires. Your choice is God's plan even when He is not moving in the timing or the way you want Him to, and you hold on to the unfolding of His plan.

25. If you insert alternate plans, you do not act like it is God's plan. You admit it was your own will or yielding at word.

26. When people recognize your transformation and holiness, inquire about it, want prayer, want God, and want transformation.

27. When people recognize your transformation and holiness and are cautious about what they do and say around you - they honor God's holiness in you.

28. When people boast about your works (deliverance, healings, miracles, signs, and wonders) and your CHARACTER! They see the nature of God in how you live and what you do for God.

29. When God honors your pursuit and heart for Him and brags to you and others about being pleased with you.

    - *1Samuel 13:14 But now thy kingdom shall not continue: the Lord hath sought him a man after his own heart, and the Lord hath commanded him to be captain over his people, because thou hast not kept that which the Lord commanded thee.*

    - *Matthew 3:17 And lo a voice from heaven, saying, This is my beloved Son, in whom I am well pleased.*

30. When God wants to use you because you are after His heart and your character and nature represents his likeness.

    - *Acts 32:22 And when he had removed him, he raised up unto them David to be their king; to whom also he gave their testimony, and said, I have found David the son of Jesse, a man after mine own heart, which shall fulfil all my will.*

    - *Matthew 17:5 While he yet spake, behold, a bright cloud overshadowed them: and behold a voice out of the cloud, which said, This is my beloved Son, in whom I am well pleased; hear ye him.*

This chapter is so vital because the warlock is coming for your desire and lifestyle of holiness.

The warlock will try to get you to compromise your holiness by making you believe it is not as sacred or necessary for your salvation.

The warlock will want you to think that holiness is not possible and will want you to focus on feeding your humanity rather than submitting it to your spirit so that God's power can sustain you.

The warlock will try to get you to believe that there are other paths to God and that God grants grace for those who do not want to or cannot sustain a life of holiness. He wants you to think grace allows you to keep sinning and still claim you love and live for God.

The warlock may engage in acts of fasting and consecration, but it will not be for holiness. It will be for power. The warlock is interested in being God. He is not interested in surrendering to God. He will dictate to you when he wants to abstain, while making sure you yield your body to him during times that are centered around his witchcraft timetables as he is sacrificing your virtue to Satan for power.

Those that may not be blatant warlocks but have succumbed to warlock workings are drawn in to pursue sexual activities at different times as seasons, while being blind to the fact that they are engaging in witchcraft sacrifices. This is the reason they call you at certain times of the month, certain days, crests, and times of the night. You think they miss you, want to get back with you;

or think it's just Netflix and chill. They are subject to the witching hours and seasons because of the open doors in their lives. You become a casualty to the trading floors of demonic altars that they are soul tied to.

Deliverance Activation

1. Study scriptures on God's holiness and spend time communing with Him through His essence of holiness. Allow him to teach you about His holiness and the reason He wants you to be holy.

2. Ask God to show you what areas of your life need to be delivered to further process you to holiness.

3. Ask God to reveal areas of compromise and work with Holy Spirit to be delivered and to set boundaries in these areas. Set three goals you can work on with Him to sanctify this area of your life.

Is The Bed Undefiled?

This chapter is important because a warlock has the tendency to draw the woman into agreeing to marital obligations and demands without legally being married or without regarding the standards and boundaries of God. The woman has the tendency to be soul tied into making these agreements and covenants without realizing that she has entered into agreements that have subjected her to all types of bewitching altars, erred ideologies, behaviors, demons, and demonic systems. If the man is not a blatant warlock but is susceptible due to open doors, he, too, does not know that he is subjecting himself or the woman to these areas. It is very important that the woman is clear about what God is saying to her directly and from His word as it relates to standards of purity. This will help her to avoid succumbing to compromises that cause drama in her life.

- Being a girlfriend, cohabiter, the other woman, or the common-law wife does not mean you are a godly covenant wife.

- Being prostituted, trafficked, a booty call, or being used for sexual acts does not make you a wife.

Warlocks like to hook women into believing that they are the love of their lives or that they will marry them. They also use words in a way that draws the woman into believing that the compromises and acts they engage in are necessary and needed for the purpose of fulfilling the needs (even sexual ones) of the warlock and the relationship. The warlock will misconstrue scripture and even use marriage terminology to lure the woman into subjecting herself to these acts. If the woman does not want to perform these acts, he may also cause her to feel as if she is less of a woman, a good for nothing woman, a woman who is not mature, not evolving, or one who is a failure at pleasing her man. Often these sexual relations are inordinate, perverted, violating, and offensive to the woman and to God.

Sometimes the warlock refers to marriage scriptures in an attempt to play on the women's emotions. He knows that the average woman wants to be married, valued, and loved by one man - her husband. The warlock will have the woman playing wifey with the promise or insinuation of marriage. Of course, his intentions are impure and only for personal gain. The warlock will sometimes tell the woman that she might as well honor him and go ahead and do what he says. He does this by convincing her to believe that because they will be getting married one day, their bed is undefiled. The warlock will have the woman honoring him like he is her husband; he presents himself in a way that causes her to be that he knows what is best for her and the relationship. The woman will posture herself in this place because as women are often taught to be submissive to men and to demonstrate this in interaction and dating. Such qualities have been deemed as factors of a good woman who is ready for marriage. By the time she realize she is engaging in these wifely duties, that she is being defiled, sacrificed, and at times even prostituted, she is so soul tied to the entanglements of the warlock that she cannot decipher the truth of God from the voice of the warlock. At this point, most women go into a *"wanting to please the man"* mode. They engage in lots of shameful acts that leave them trying to justify their submissiveness, as they only slip further into the depths of drowning in the hookings of the warlock.

Let's explore revelation on the undefiled bed so we can be clear about what the Bible says. This will aide in helping us to realize that we are becoming prey to the subtle religious jargon and scriptures used to manipulate us.

Hebrews 13:14 *Marriage is honourable in all, and the bed undefiled: but whoremongers and adulterers God will judge.*

The Amplified Bible *Let marriage be held in honor (esteemed worthy, precious, of great price, and especially dear) in all things. And thus let the marriage bed be undefiled (kept undishonored); for God will judge and punish the unchaste [all guilty of sexual vice] and adulterous.*

Undefiled is *amiantos* in Greek and means:
1. unsoiled, i.e. (figuratively) pure: — undefiled
2. not defiled, free from that by which the nature of a thing is deformed and debased, or its force and vigor impaired

Dictionary.com defines *undishonored* as:
1. lack or loss of honor; disgraceful or dishonest character or conduct
2. disgrace; ignominy; shame
3. an indignity; insult
4. a cause of shame or disgrace
5. to deprive of honor; disgrace; bring reproach or shame on
6. to rape or seduce

We'd like to think an undefiled bed means we can do what we desire because we are married or are in a relationship that has the potential for marriage. But if there is sexual interaction outside of wedlock or, if there are acts that bring shame, dishonor, reproach, and disgrace upon a partner and upon God, then the bed is subject to defilement. If we are making our partners engage in acts that they are uncomfortable with, especially if there are areas of their soul and identity that need to be healed regarding intimacy, we could be defiling the marriage bed. As we examine the definitions, some acts could be considered rape when there is seduction in the form of manipulation and control rather than in the form of *Eros love* and a desire to romanticize your mate. Thus, we could be subjecting the marriage bed to defilement.

When defilement enters the marriage bed or a relationship, we are operating in *Aheb love* rather than *Eros love*.

- *Aheb love* can be an inordinate love rooted in physical attraction, lust, ungodly cravings, perversion, vain imaginations, demonization, and erred doctrine, where the person is engaging in relationship interactions and sexual acts that are sinful, wicked, rooted in man's flesh, or that disregard the boundaries of God.

- *Eros love* is a romantic love, admiration, esteem, passion, and attraction between a woman and a man. It is the love a man or a woman have for a partner of the opposite sex that they romantically admire and would desire to marry. Eros love is often misconstrued and even tainted with lust. Even though it is a healthy innate love, if Eros love is not

113

properly governed or filtered through a pure mind, heart, and soul, it can cause people to fall into fornication, adultery, inappropriate sexual or lustful behaviors. This type of love is intended for marriage and should not be intricately engaged or ignited outside of matrimony. After marriage, Eros love can be fully awakened, and is essential for the wellness of sexual intimacy, and the strengthening of the relationship bond within the marriage covenant.

Aheb love will have us succumbing to a love that is driven more by perversion than the innate desires of sex and intimacy that God instilled in us.

Many people believe purity means abstaining and self-control, but purity means sanctification.

1Thessalonians 4:3-4 For this is the will of God, even your sanctification, that ye should abstain from fornication: That every one of you should know how to possess his vessel in sanctification and honour.

<u>Sanctification</u> in Greek is *hagiasmos* and means:
1. purification, i.e. (the state) purity
2. concretely (by Hebraism) a purifier
3. holiness, sanctification, consecration
4. the effect of consecration
5. sanctification of heart and life

Sanctification is about being restored in innocence, holiness, and purity according to the standard and will of God.

Sanctification is a state of separation unto God. As we are separated unto God, we are able to abstain.

All believers enter into an initial state of sanctification when they are born of God. Sanctification is not possible outside of God's presence, relationship, and will, as a person cannot purify themselves. Neither is there anything apart from God that can make a person acceptable unto Him. A person must continue to glory in His presence and in covenant with Him if they are to continue to evolve in sanctification with Him.

1Corinthians 1:29-31 That no flesh should glory in his presence. But of him are ye in Christ Jesus, who of God is made unto us wisdom, and righteousness, and sanctification, and redemption: That, according as it is written, He that glorieth, let him glory in the Lord.

Jesus did not come to save our flesh, but to save our spirit. There must be a relinquishing of flesh to produce sanctification. When having to give up sin for sanctification, our flesh will always war for gratification – it wars against the spirit of God in us.

Flesh is going to be flesh; it will never be happy about having to die inside God's presence, not being able to be fed by what it desires. It will only want sanctification when it has died inside of God and has risen in resurrection power by being crucified unto Christ Jesus.

Galatians 5:17 For the flesh lusteth against the Spirit, and the Spirit against the flesh: and these are contrary the one to the other: so that ye cannot do the things that ye would.

Romans. 7:15-23 For that which I do I allow not: for what I would, that do I not; but what I hate, that do I. If then I do that which I would not, I consent unto the law that it is good. Now then it is no more I that do it, but sin that dwelleth in me. For I know that in me (that is, in my flesh,) dwelleth no good thing: for to will is present with me; but how to perform that which is good I find not. For the good that I would I do not: but the evil which I would not, that I do. Now if I do that I would not, it is no more I that do it, but sin that dwelleth in me. I find then a law, that, when I would do good, evil is present with me. For I delight in the law of God after the inward man: But I see another law in my members, warring against the law of my mind, and bringing me into captivity to the law of sin which is in my members

When our flesh wars against our spirit, it feels as if we're being punished and as if being saved is a drag, rather than viewing sanctification as a needful blessing that demonstrates God's love and likeness.

2Thessalonians 2:13 But we ought always to thank God for you, brothers and sisters loved by the Lord, because God chose you as firstfruits to be saved through the sanctifying work of the Spirit and through belief in the truth.

2Timothy 2:21 Those who cleanse themselves from the latter will be instruments for special purposes, made holy, useful to the Master and prepared to do any good work.

Galatians 2:20 I have been crucified with Christ and I no longer live, but Christ lives in me. The life I now live in the body, I live by faith in the Son of God, who loved me and gave himself for me.

116

Hebrews 9:14 How much more, then, will the blood of Christ, who through the eternal Spirit offered himself unblemished to God, cleanse our consciences from acts that lead to death, so that we may serve the living God!

Sanctification provides discipline, self-control, temperance, boundaries, wellness, and peace.
Sanctification enables us to serve God in worship, praise, offerings, sacrifice, spiritual works, and ministry.

Sanctification protects us from:

- ✓ Carnality, ideologies, and behaviors that do not please God
- ✓ Heartbreak and trauma
- ✓ Unnecessary bondages and experiences
- ✓ Soul ties (as sex is spiritual); when we have sexual encounters, our souls are tied to those we sleep with
- ✓ Bondages, transferences, demonization, and spiritual attacks that come from being soul tied.
- ✓ Addictions, perversions, and sexual propensities, that come from being soul tied to others.
- ✓ Memories that draw us back into or cause us to relive sin, heartbreak, and trauma

Anytime we justify not being sanctified, we have not matured with God. This is an indication that we have not pursued God's presence, developed a relationship with His Holy Spirit, and have not consistently studied His word as a lifestyle, so that sanctification of purity, righteousness, and holiness is birthed, cultivated, and evolved in us – formed in us.

Do you want Christ to be formed in you?

Galatians 4:19 My little children, of whom I travail in birth
again until Christ be formed in you.

In the previous chapter, we learned that holiness requires us
to be broken and contrite until we become a living
sacrifice. Now we are learning that sanctification requires
us to travail. *Travail* means "*toiling, pain, labor, exertion,
anguish or suffering resulting from mental or physical
hardship, the pain of childbirth.*"

As we think about how being ridden of sin can feel like a
drag or punishment, we recognize that there is a time of
unpleasant work that must be done to produce and sustain
us in this sanctification. Sanctification is freely given to us
but requires a toiling to manifest its fullness in us as a
lifestyle. Many do not want to do the work that leads to
their being fashioned in Christ. This is how the warlock
and other enticers draw us away from God.

Let me pose it a different way!

When we say we believe in Jesus Christ and His works on
the Cross, we are actually declaring that we are dying to sin
and are rising in eternal life with Him. When we accept
this as our truth, sanctification enters our lives.
Sanctification is actually the blood of Jesus and His
experience on the Cross. Relinquishing ourselves of sin
causes the exchanging of sanctification. Then we must
enter a cross experience – fellowship in His suffering –
while being resurrected unto God through holiness,
sanctification, and righteousness. The work was done over

118

2000 years ago with Jesus Christ, but we must manifest and live out the work in our own lives.

Until we walk out a consecration season and live it as our truth, we will never love and joy in sanctification. We will always deem it an unattainable burden that steals our fun in life. We will always think that grace is giving us a pass to sin, when grace really means power to overcome sin. Such erred doctrine will have us claiming salvation, misrepresenting God, operating through a form of godliness, yet left with open doors that allow manipulation by warlocks, enticers, demons, and demonic systems.

Deliverance Activation

1. Journal what you learned about this chapter. Include every misconception you had regarding salvation and sanctification.
2. Study the scriptures in this chapter. Spend time journaling what you learned from them so you can truly have clarity about God's salvation and sanctification.
3. Journal the reason sanctification needs to be birthed in you and what you need to do to submit to a season of being consecrated until Christ is birthed in you.
4. Being contrite, broken, and travailing requires a humility where you die to self and rise in God. Journal what needs to bow in you in order to SHIFT into consistently living in this posture.
5. Journal three goals you can work on to produce this bowing where you begin to birth forth true sanctification.

Building Strong Covenant With God

Often times we cannot identify or enter into a true covenant relationship because we were focused on the fruits of fame, fortune, blessings, works, gifting, gimmicks, signs and wonders. We deem these as indicators of God's presence and approval. However, a strong covenant relationship with God SHIFTS us beyond religion, works, worldliness, and what we are accustomed to experiencing in our relationships with people. A covenant relationship with God allows Him to be the center and head of our lives and the only Governor and Ruler of our lives with everything about our lives coming through and being approved of by Him.

God desires us to build a lasting relationship with Him, where such communion becomes our lifestyle. (Attributes below are from my *"Sustaining The Vision Workbook)."*

Deliverance Activation

Spend time studying the following attributes and scriptures. Journal where you need to grow in your covenant relationship with God.

1. **Communication** - communicating your thoughts, feelings and desires to God, allowing Him to do the same. Be open to constructive criticism and to changing for the better of oneself and the relationship.

2. **Honesty** - Be honest in your communication, even about your fears, hurts, pains, joys, what you do not agree with, what you need clarity for or patience with, etc. If God urgently needs something from you, He will equip you or reveal to you how you are already equipped. Otherwise, you will find Him to be a patient God who is willing to journey in the process with you. You must be honest, so His grace can prevail where your pride and insecurity have caused you to surrender to leaning on and trusting in Him.

3. **Vulnerability** - Please know that communication = vulnerability. There is no way to communicate effectively without being vulnerable. Striving to protect ourselves from rejection, hurt, and disappointment only causes more agony and consequences than being vulnerable would. I say this because we risk losing or never obtaining the very thing we say we want. We fail to give ourselves a voice and opportunity to have our needs and desires met.

   ***Psalm 138:8** The LORD will perfect that which concerneth me: thy mercy, O LORD, endureth for ever: forsake not the works of thine own hands*

4. **Trust** - When God says He will never leave or forsake you, He means it. You can take God at His word. It never returns void. The key is to be in alignment, to connect with His word as it comes to pass. And even when you miss it, God

will provide opportunities for you to connect with His word again. He wants you to receive what He has for you. Trust shifts us to a place where obedience is not a chore but is a desire and the choice to have confidence in the will of God for our lives and for what we say we desire out of life. *Deuteronomy 31:6 Be strong and of a good courage, fear not, nor be afraid of them: for the LORD thy God, he it is that doth go with thee; he will not fail thee, nor forsake thee.*

5. **Respect** - Respect demonstrates a conscious honor, reverence, gratitude and consideration for another. We tend to respect people based on their positions, abilities, beliefs, etc., but God requires us to also respect one another simply because we exist together. God requires us to respect Him and His position as our God, and to honor and respect Him by keeping His commandments. *1John 2:5 But if anyone obeys his word, love for God is truly made complete in them. This is how we know we are in him.*

6. **Patience** - Just like you need God to be patient with you, you must be patient with God. Often, we perceive patience as not getting what we want when we want it. Patience is a fruit of the spirit and a fruit starts out as a seed that grows into a fruit. Patience is the ability to grow into something with someone or grow towards a goal or desire. To watch a seed blossom into what it is going to be, requires cultivation. This is where you are able to further work your relationship with God and with what you are

waiting on. You are able to go deeper in communion where you walk with Him in uncomfortable times, times of expectation, and times of uncertainty, while what you are waiting on flourishes into that which you receive or achieve.

7. **Quality Time** - is time spent in giving another one's undivided attention in order to strengthen a relationship. Quality time can be simply resting in the presence of God as it can be communicative or no communication. We always want God to talk but this qualifies only as a relationship of performance rather than a balanced relationship where every facet of the relationship is developed, cultivated, and prospering. *Revelations 3:20 Behold, I stand at the door, and knock: if any man hear my voice, and open the door, I will come in to him, and will sup with him, and he with me.*

8. **Agreement & Covenant Cooperation** – Our entire relationship with God is about restoring and resting in the covenant that was originally ours before the fall of Adam and Eve. We must come into agreement with that covenant and allow God to lead us into the truth, grace, wellness, protection, and prosperity that is rightfully ours. Our agreement must be verbal. It also must manifest through our daily actions and submitted posture to whom God has created us to be in the earth.

9. **Individuality Appreciation** - Often we are challenged by God's uniqueness because we do not understand it. When we think we have a grasp on who He is, He unveils another level of Himself. This should not intimidate or frustrate us because if we really consider ourselves - if we are truly walking in alignment and relationship with the Lord, we, also, are always evolving and changing. The deliverance, healing, and building of ourselves into the character and nature of God, should continuously transform us into the standard of God. We must appreciate how He evolves and reveals Himself to us, how we evolve and reveal ourselves to the world, and how others evolve and reveal themselves to us and the world.

10. **Praise & Worship Empowerment** - Praise and worship opens a portal that mirrors God's image and likeness back to you. The more you exalt God in who He is, the more He unveils who you are to Him and to the world. Empower yourself through personal praise and worship, corporate praise and worship, and in allowing yours to be a lifestyle of ministry unto God.

11. **Lifelong Learner** – Possess a desire to know God and what pleases Him. The reason we pray, study the Word, and other materials about God is because we want to know Him – learn of him. Become a lifelong learner so that all there is to know about your evolving God can be revealed to you.

12. **Accountability** - Be accountable to cultivating the relationship and to the promises and vows you make with God and with others. Do not make vows you cannot keep. If you struggle keeping them, repent quickly and seek God for the deliverance and healing needed to keep the vows. You can also ask God to provide steps you can commit to, such that you work towards fulfilling the vows.

13. **Fidelity** - Be faithful to the relationship you have with God. Do not put things, people, situations, life pursuits, and idols in the place of God or ahead of God.

14. **Freewill** - God does not force us into relationship with Him. He allows the right to choose. God would rather be heartbroken, not having relationship with us, rather than be dysfunctional, forcing us into a relationship that we do not want to be in.

15. **SHIFT** – SHIFT to loving God with all your heart, all your mind, and all your soul. Do not fret! You will get there as you work on walking with Him daily and letting Him guide you in your destiny lifestyle. YOU GOT THIS! SHIFT!

Isaiah 1:21-23 How is the faithful city become an harlot! it was full of judgment; righteousness lodged in it; but now murderers. Thy silver is become dross, thy wine mixed with water: Thy princes are rebellious, and companions of thieves: every one loveth gifts, and followeth after rewards:

they judge not the fatherless, neither doth the cause of the widow come unto them.

Matthew 7:22-23 Many will say to me in that day, Lord, Lord, have we not prophesied in thy name? and in thy name have cast out devils? and in thy name done many wonderful works? And then will I profess unto them, I never knew you: depart from me, ye that work iniquity.

Matthew 24:24 For false Christs and false prophets will arise and will show great signs and wonders, so as to mislead, if possible, even the elect.

Luke 16:13 No servant can serve two masters: for either he will hate the one, and love the other; or else he will hold to the one, and despise the other. Ye cannot serve God and mammon

John 14:27 Peace I leave with you; my peace I give to you. Not as the world gives do I give to you. Let not your hearts be troubled, neither let them be afraid.

John 16:33 I have told you these things so that in Me you may have peace. In the world you will have tribulation. But take courage; I have overcome the world!"

2Thessalonians 2:3-9 Let no man deceive you by any means: for that day shall not come, except there come a falling away first, and that man of sin be revealed, the son of perdition; Who opposeth and exalteth himself above all that is called God, or that is worshipped; so that he as God sitteth in the temple of God, shewing himself that he is God. Remember ye not, that, when I was yet with you, I told you these things? And now ye know what withholdeth that he might be revealed in his time. For the mystery of iniquity doth already work: only he who now letteth will let, until he be taken out of the way. And then shall that Wicked be revealed, whom the Lord shall consume with the spirit of his mouth, and shall destroy with the brightness of his coming: Even him, whose coming is after the working of Satan with all power and signs and lying wonders.

***James 1:26-27** The Amplified Bible If anyone thinks himself to be religious (piously observant of the external duties of his faith) and does not bridle his tongue but deludes his own heart, this person's religious service is worthless (futile, barren). External religious worship [religion as it is expressed in outward acts] that is pure and unblemished in the sight of God the Father is this: to visit and help and care for the orphans and widows in their affliction and need, and to keep oneself unspotted and uncontaminated from the world.*

***James 3:1-6** Go to now, ye rich men, weep and howl for your miseries that shall come upon you. Your riches are corrupted, and your garments are motheaten. Your gold and silver is cankered; and the rust of them shall be a witness against you, and shall eat your flesh as it were fire. Ye have heaped treasure together for the last days. Behold, the hire of the labourers who have reaped down your fields, which is of you kept back by fraud, crieth: and the cries of them which have reaped are entered into the ears of the Lord of sabaoth. Ye have lived in pleasure on the earth, and been wanton; ye have nourished your hearts, as in a day of slaughter. Ye have condemned and killed the just; and he doth not resist you.*

James 4:4 *You adulteresses! Do you not know that friendship with the world is hostility toward God? Therefore, whoever chooses to be a friend of the world renders himself an enemy of God.*

1John 2:15 *Love not the world, neither the things that are in the world. If any man love the world, the love of the Father is not in him.*

Romans 12:2 *And be not conformed to this world: but be ye transformed by the renewing of your mind, that ye may prove what is that good, and acceptable, and perfect, will of God.*

1Corinthians 1:21-25 *For after that in the wisdom of God the world by wisdom knew not God, it pleased God by the foolishness of preaching to save them that believe. For the Jews require a sign, and the Greeks seek after wisdom: But we preach Christ crucified, unto the Jews a stumbling block, and unto the Greeks foolishness; But unto them which are called, both Jews and Greeks, Christ the power of God, and the wisdom of God. Because the foolishness of God is wiser than men; and the weakness of God is stronger than men.*

Avoiding Warlock Trauma

To avoid warlock trauma, I encourage women to implement the following strategy.

WE ARE NOT HAVING IT!

- Have a strong uncompromising covenant relationship with God such that you are sold out to Him. Know how to identify this in others versus pretenders.

- Ask God for revelation and insight regarding the man's purpose for entering your life. This needs to be done at the initial onset of the entry. Knowing the person's purpose will enable you to keep proper boundaries, not engage in roles that God did not ordain or that may not be in the timing of God.

- Do not approach every man as a potential husband or romantic relationship. This behavior closes off the opportunity to simply have male acquaintances and friendships. Thinking of every man as a potential mate, also opens the door to be swooned by crafty men.

- Know your destiny and calling; Know the type of husband you desire; Know the standards you need to maintain and that he needs to possess in order to aide you in sustaining your God identity, virtue, destiny, and evolving purpose.

Isaiah 59:19 *So shall they fear the name of the Lord from the west, and his glory from the rising of the sun. When the enemy shall come in like a flood, the Spirit of the Lord shall lift up a standard against him.*

<u>*Standard* is *nus* in Hebrew and means:</u>
1. to flit (to move lightly and swiftly, fly, change one's address)
2. vanish away (subside, escape; causatively, chase, impel, deliver) (disappear quickly, make invisible, disappear by ceasing to exist; come to an end)
3. abate (annul, extinguish, suppress), away, be displayed, (make to) flee (away,- ing)
4. put to flight, hide, lift up a standard, • to drive hastily, to cause to disappear, hide.

When we know God's standard and STAND in it, our standard becomes the weapon we need to abate, send fleeing, drive away, and vanish. We put an end to the challenging or potentially fiery trials in our lives.

A standard is an approved model. In this case, it is a model approved by God which guarantees that it aligns with His word and will.

<u>Dictionary.com defines *standard* as:</u>
1. something considered by an authority or by general consent as a basis of comparison
2. a rule or principle that is used as a basis for judgment
3. an average or normal requirement, quality, quantity, level, grade, etc.
4. standards, those morals, ethics, habits, etc.

5. established by authority, custom, or an individual as acceptable

Spend time with God in identifying and journaling your standards. Practice engaging with men through your standards and live them as a lifestyle.

- Know the characteristics of a godly man and how those standards compare to your personal standards required for a mate. The Bible says we know a person by their fruit.

   Mathew 7:16-20 Ye shall know them by their fruits. Do men gather grapes of thorns, or figs of thistles? Even so every good tree bringeth forth good fruit; but a corrupt tree bringeth forth evil fruit. A good tree cannot bring forth evil fruit, neither can a corrupt tree bring forth good fruit. Every tree that bringeth not forth good fruit is hewn down, and cast into the fire. Wherefore by their fruits ye shall know them.

Trust the fruit of what the person shows you.

- Do not compromise based on potential. Know the difference between working potential and pretending. Trust the reality of the person. Be empowered by reality and do not swoon by potential.

- Have non-negotiables, especially in the areas of abuse, control, neglect, narcissism, and blatant sin.

- Get healed of past traumas regarding relationships. Attend counseling if necessary. Do not use relationships to heal unless God is revealing that this is one of the purposes for the relationship. Work on being healed before entering relationships; especially begin healed of man and father issues. Evolve in relationship with God and know get to know Him as Lord, Savior, and Father so that these roles are already healed in your soul and identity.

- Know personal and generational behavioral patterns, open doors, and cycles. Know the boundaries and standards needed to keep them closed. Do not compromise in this area. Pursue deliverance and inner healing in order to break strongholds in these areas.

- Consider a slow appropriate pace when building a relationship; allow acquaintanceship and friendship to evolve and then build from a healthy foundation.

- Implement heathy emotional, interpersonal, social, communication, anger management, and conflict resolution skills. Be open to learning and implementing these skills into the foundation of the relationship with the person. If the person is unwilling to evolve in healthy relationship skills, consider this a red flag when considering whether to pursue further would be beneficial. There is no way to truly build a healthy relationship without these skills.

- Do not assume that men not approaching you means that something is wrong with you. Sometimes the Lord places His hedge of protection around His chosen, so they do not succumb to the trappings of the enemy. Job had a hedge around him.

Job 1:8-10 The Amplified Bible And the Lord said to Satan, Have you considered My servant Job, that there is none like him on the earth, a blameless and upright man, one who [reverently] fears God and abstains from and shuns evil [because it is wrong]? Then Satan answered the Lord, Does Job [reverently] fear God for nothing? Have You not put a hedge about him and his house and all that he has, on every side? You have conferred prosperity and happiness upon him in the work of his hands, and his possessions have increased in the land.

Many women assume they are cursed, unapproachable, or too this or that. I have been told that I am too modest, too covered up, that I have standards that are too high, that I do not go out of the house enough, that I am too focused on God, too anointed, and on and on. I have been told these lies by Christian women. The women tried to encourage me to show cleavage, wear shorter skirts and dresses, dumb myself down regarding spiritual matters and how God uses me. They told me to slow down on doing the work of the Lord, and on and on the erred wisdom goes. God would quickly rebuke me and let me know that none of this folly is of Him; that my lack of being pursued has nothing to do with anything I needed to break, cast out, or change about myself. In many seasons it has simply been His wall of protection around me. In other seasons God simply has been jealous for me and have not wanted to share my time and attention.

Many of these women judged me without realizing that as a single woman it was scriptural for me to care for the things of God.

1Corinthians 7:34 There is difference also between a wife and a virgin. The unmarried woman careth for the things of the Lord, that she may be holy both in body and in spirit: but she that is married careth for the things of the world, how she may please her husband.

The word *careth* means *"to take thought, have care, be anxious about, be careful about."* Such a care is a conscious and needful pursuit. The Word of God says it enables the single woman to be holy in body and in spirit. This pursuit is a protection in and of itself for when the unmarried woman is caring for the things of God, it consecrates her to only want, be, and do, what pleases God. It also keeps her in communion with Him so warlocks cannot prey on her singleness.

Also, God has told me that some men know who they can approach and who they cannot. Men know who they can try and what women they will not be able to get over on.

James 1:14-15 The Amplified Bible But every person is tempted when he is drawn away, enticed and baited by his own evil desire (lust, passions). Then the evil desire, when it has conceived, gives birth to sin, and sin, when it is fully matured, brings forth death.

2Peter 18:19 For when they speak great swelling words of vanity, they allure through the lusts of the flesh, through much wantonness, those that were clean escaped from them who live in error. While they promise them liberty, they themselves are the servants of corruption: for of whom a man is overcome, of the same is he brought in bondage.

134

Some men, especially those who are offenders or are looking for prey for personal gain, are able to identify gullible, victimized, insecure, impure, perverse women. When a woman is clear in her identity, calling, and are grounded in God, a man who is not in alignment with God will be less likely to flirt with her or approach her. If a woman has purified herself unto righteousness, there will be nothing within her that is in common with lustful, perverse, compromising, sinful men. There may simply not be any men with the same God likeness that she has, so the men around her will not be drawn to her pure fruit because they lack it. Additionally, the men who are purified unto righteousness may have a certain woman God requires for them, and she simply does not fit the standard.

Some men are intimidated by successful women. Women are more successful and advancing than they have ever been in life. This will only increase as women are provided more opportunities to evolve educationally, entrepreneurially, and economically. Insecure men will find it difficult to come along side of a successful woman and lead and cover her in destiny. Communication with God is so vital in avoiding the false perceptions that may potentially remove the hedge of God or that may cause a woman to engage in acts that draw the attention that God is blocking or that their consecration is preventing.

- Have those in your life who can help keep you accountable to your standards, encourage and support you in your waiting, and aide you in navigating relations in a godly manner as men SHIFT into your life. Do not disconnect from your accountability partners. Do not allow men to separate you from your accountability partner. This is a huge red flag of a warlock operation. Such warlocks are generationally abusers, controlling, or narcissistic. Loneliness, helplessness, depression, fear, shame, and condemnation tends to cause great mental and psychological warfare. This oppression makes it difficult to gain a sense of empowerment in breaking free from a warlock situation when disconnecting from your support system. Supports aide in being the safeguards and lifeguards that crush warlock hookings.

Safety Activation

As you engage in relationships with men, refer to this chapter as a safeguard for how to maintain balance and keep yourself protected. Make sure you have already identified and learned the following:

- Your calling
- Your standards for yourself and a mate
- Healthy relationship skills
- Clarity on reality versus potential
- Clarity on the fruit of the spirit
- Accountability partners whom you trust and are in daily covenant with where separation isn't an option
- Strong covenant with God
- Healed of past trauma
- Clarity on how to keep doors closed to ungodly patterns, cycles, and behavior.

Deliverance From The Fixer Spirit

Women are innately,

✓ Inventors
✓ Birthers
✓ Intercessors
✓ Deliverers
✓ Producers
✓ Reproducers
✓ Nurturers
✓ Saviors
✓ Cultivators
✓ Releasers

These qualities
automatically cause
them to want to draw the
from anyone and
anything they encounter.

Due to the shortage of Christian men in the church and the absenteeism of fathers in the home, women have had to take on roles that were innately designed for men. This has sometimes caused the role of the woman in relationships to become blurred where they tend to be more in their lives and the lives of men than God intended.

Though we are to build a man in the sense of building him up, we are not supposed to fix him where he feels like he is being recreated all over again.

Let me say it another way:

It is essential and necessary to be empowered, a support, an encourager and a helper to those we date. It is unhealthy to engage in behaviors of fixing a man.

Some women become so obsessed with "fixing the man" that they lose themselves. The man literally becomes a project. Although some of what the woman is suggesting, or imparting is needful or beneficial, the man will start to resent the woman's actions because it makes him feel inadequate, insufficient, unsuitable, and void of his manhood.

Though we can share our standards and desires, and though a man may take the initiative to work with God so he can evolve in these areas, never should we try to force fit men into a mold or standard in an effort to make them "the God-sent one" in our lives.

It is also acceptable to suggest improvements that encourage a man to SHIFT into a greater likeness of God identity and destiny attainment where he becomes the reality of his potential, but we should never become God in his life such that we are dictating his transformation.

Truth is, we should not want more or do more for people than they want or are willing to do for themselves. A man should be so with us to the point where he is smitten or provoked to improve himself because of who we are. When we work harder than he does to get him to work his potential, we have become a fixer. This does not mean that a man cannot become stuck in a rut or find

138

himself in a challenging space needing to be pulled out as hard seasons are a part of life. But when we do not face the reality that this is his personality, we take on the full-time job of molding him into the man we want and end up finding that we have crossed into the danger zone.

Such a role can be tedious, draining, dreadful, discouraging, confusing, and contentious. The man will war against the fixer in you, which can only lead to constant conflict, frustration, disrespect, rejection, dejection, hurt, and wounding. Where you should be building one another up, you end up tearing one another down.

Much of the way a fixer operates is through intentional or unintentional witchcraft as the woman is seeking to illegally manipulate the free will of a person. I am going to share revelation about the fixer from my *"Healing The Wounded Leader"* manual. Use this information to assess fixer behaviors and mentalities and seek deliverance from how the fixer spirit causes you to ultimately find yourself navigating as a warlocking witch.

Please note that this is a broad revelation of the fixer spirit. Some may not possess all these qualities but may still be bound by the fixer spirit.

Dictionary.com defines *fixer* as:
1. a person or thing that fixes
2. Informal. a person who arranges matters in advance through bribery or influence

Dictionary.com defines *fix* as:
1. to repair; mend

2. to put in order or in good condition; adjust or arrange
3. to make fast, firm, or stable
4. to place definitely and more or less permanently
5. to settle definitely; determine
6. to direct (the eyes, the attention, etc.) steadily
7. to attract and hold (the eye, the attention, etc.).
8. to make set or rigid
9. to put into permanent form
10. to put or place (responsibility, blame, etc.) on a person

A fixer has a driven need to repair, rescue, or help someone while attempting to fit the person into their personal perception of how they believe someone should be, what they feel would perfect the person or the person's life. The fixer tends to bombard the person with their own ideas and perceptions of what the fixer believes it will take to make the person perfect. The fixer also tends to only accept the person if the person conforms to the fixer's perceptions, eventually yielding to what the fixer believes it will take to perfect the person's life.

A fixer can also be someone who has the best interest of others at heart. The fixer sees a person's potential, but cares more about the person changing than the person cares about it themselves. Such a person (fixer) ends up playing roles in the person's life that they should not. The fixer resorts to being more to the person than they should be.

The fixer is striving to be the rescuer and although some of their perceptions can be useful and beneficial, the well through which these ideas are filtered, is usually by way of negativity, a critical mess, a need to control, a need to be needed and a need to fix others. Most fixers have unresolved hurts, painful pasts or challenging experiences and as a result, they use their fixer mindset in an effort to rescue others from hardship.

Some fixers fear being hurt due to unresolved issues from their past. This leads to their striving to perfect those who desire relationship with them. The challenge to this (for the fixer) is that they now try to make the person consistently fix things about themselves in order to please the fixer so the person can remain a part of the fixer's life. By the time the person fixes one thing about themselves, the fixer has already presented another thing to fix. The person finds themselves constantly jumping through hoops to try and please the fixer. However, the fixer cannot be pleased because their issue is actually not that person, but the fixer's own need to be healed. They engage in their relationships through their past unhealed pains and fears of being hurt again.

Some fixers have the heart and compassion of God, the gift of discernment and helps and the gift of administration. They are called to lead, shepherd, train and equip people, yet they use their gifts in an unhealthy or unbalanced manner. They end up becoming God and/or an enabler in peoples' lives. Their need or drive to be the savior of the person causes them to be more to the person than God has said, or it causes them to take on more than God is requiring. This type of fixer possesses great positive qualities and giftings but needs balance in making sure they are allowing God to be God. If they allow God to be God, they will not end up hating their lives and callings and resenting those whom they are called to help as a result of becoming and bearing more than God has intended.

Fixers tend to build a lifestyle of false peace and false perfection. They do this by holding on to people through superficial and surface relationships. If you penetrate their walls, you will find some mental instabilities and inabilities to truly trust, relax, and rest in the love and security of the relationship.

Anytime you are imperfect, the fixer takes this as a personal attack against themselves. They view your downfalls as your hurting them, betraying them, and dishonoring them, especially if they gave you advice on a matter but you did not implement it or were not consistent in utilizing it. *"How dare you not take their advice and run with it."* The fixer tends to punish the person by ending the relationship or threatening to end it, if the person does not correct this betrayal immediately.

The fixer will also use silence and abusive threats to control and manipulate a person into feeling guilty and ashamed of not following through with their advice. The person will often feel beat down, condemned, confused and double-minded by the negative words and negative perceptions that the fixer speaks towards them. The person will feel confused and double-minded because what the fixer says or is suggesting may have a point of truth, but the method is all wrong. Therefore, the person wavers between wanting to submit and rebelling against what the fixer is suggesting. Also, unless the person does everything the fixer says, the fixer negates any progress the person makes. It is usually all or nothing for a fixer, so the person tends to be abusively corrected and chastened despite any progress they have made.

There are instances where the fixer will obtain information about the person's past failures, and then when the fixer is correcting and chastising the person, the fixer will belittle the person reminding them of these failures. Fixers use these failures to cause the person to feel as if they will never change and will never have success if they do not adhere to what is being demanded of them.

Sometimes the fixer's perceptions of the person are rooted in their own past hurtful experiences with other people. The fixer, however, casts these perceptions onto the person, and assumes that the person is also that way, even if the person is in no way similar to the person that hurt the fixer.

A fixer checks up on the person to ensure that the person is doing what is demanded of them. The fixer will also ask certain questions in an effort to get the person to admit that they have not changed or have not followed through with what was requested. The fixer tends to attack the person's character placing the person in a position of having to defend themselves. Fear causes the person to lie in order to avoid being rebuked or shut down all together if they have not done what was required of them. Any of these positions causes the fixer to become angry and feel betrayed. What follows is usually verbally abusive or controlling manipulative acts for the purpose of forcing the person into subjection to the fixer's demands.

Though the fixer appears to celebrate you when you achieve success from doing what you were told to do, the fixer's motive of celebration is not due to your being transformed but it's because you implemented the fixer's ideas. You will recognize this when the fixer takes credit

143

for your achievement even though you did the work. The fixer will contend that you only acquired victory because of them, and without them you are a failure waiting to happen. Because fixers view themselves as the helper, it is very difficult to get them to pursue deliverance and healing from their fixer mindset. If they do acknowledge their issues, it is generally with the mindset that the only reason they are broken is because of the person they are fixing; they feel that if they fix you, that fixes them.

The fixer relationship tends to resemble Jezebel and Ahab from the bible. To Jezebel, Ahab was inadequate. She was always using control, fear, manipulation, threats, murder, and negative methods to fix situations that King Ahab had reign over (*1Kings 18-19*).

Because of the emotional soul ties and bewitchment that occurs between the fixer and the fixee, it can take years before the fixee realizes they are being abused and needs to end the relationship. The fixee has close calls of ending it but tends to talk themselves out of it when rewarded with the fixer's attention and seductive accolades The fixer make the fixee believe that these accolades are due to the fixee's good behavior in submitting to what was required of them. However, the fixers behaviors soon return and the fixees are entangled again and striving to comprehend whether the confusion and chastising they are receiving is actually abuse and unhealthy to their overall wellbeing.

The fixer can also possess many good qualities that make the fixee want to work on the relationship, to please the fixer, and even prove themselves to the fixer. The fixer tends to have the person so bewitched that the person feels as though they will be losing out by ending the relationship.

The fixee ends up feeling that they are hopeless and cannot life without the fixer. These very misconceptions are what keep the cycle of the relationship going. Eventually, the fixer tends to leave the relationship with regret, feeling that years of their life have been wasted on something that never could have been healthy; they feel that they have lost themselves in a relationship that bred only unhealthiness and identity theft.

Some of us have become fixers or have been groomed as fixers through our family roles and traditions. We have been the smart ones, the successful ones, the responsible ones or the reliable ones in the family. We have been the oldest kid, the family curse breaker, or have had to step up due to insufficient parental roles in the family. Some have had to rely on themselves and take care of others, particularly siblings. Thus, we have been molded and shaped into the fixers.

Some of us have become successful and have felt obligated to go back and fix or take care of capable family members. We feel obligated because they are family and now there is the unrealistic pressure to take care of them or enable them. This fixer mentality has been groomed within us due to the wounds of a difficult childhood, false or unhealthy cultural obligations, guilt and shame of being successful while other family members remain in poverty or role reversals where the child has had to be the parent or has had to fulfill parental duties as a child or teenager. This is not your burden to bear. Let God lead you as to when you are to assist and help your family. Do not engage in savior roles that only God can fulfill. God is the only fixer and He has promised that if we walk with Him, He will perfect (make sound) the things which concern us.

Psalm 138:8 The Lord will perfect (make sound) that which concerneth me: thy mercy, O LORD, endureth for ever: forsake not the works of thine own hands.

<u>Deliverance From A Relationship With A Fixer:</u>

1. Break the soul ties between you and the fixer.
2. Break word curses and bewitchment used through words.
3. Cleanse yourself of confusion, double mindedness, helplessness, hopelessness and a need to please and prove yourself to the fixer.
4. Break and cleanse the powers of shame, guilt and condemnation.
5. Reclaim your identity.
6. Forgive yourself for yielding to the fixer relationship.
7. Forgive the fixer for abusing you.
8. Reestablish God as the head and fixer of your life and let Him work with you on what needs to be changed in you.
9. Work on building your self-esteem and self-worth so that you do not succumb to this type of relationship ever again.

<u>Deliverance From The Fixer Mentality:</u>

1. Acknowledge you are a fixer and need deliverance and healing.
2. Explore underlying issues to fixer behaviors and receive deliverance and healing in those areas.
3. Explore and receive healing in areas related to fear of being hurt and a need to control your life and the lives of others.
4. Repent for fixer behaviors and how they have impacted others.
5. Explore your gifts of discernment, healing, and helps, and how to use them in a healthy manner.
6. Reestablish God as the head of your life and submit to His leading.
7. Work on building your trust and faith in God, so you can trust him to lead you in your relationships.

REFERENCES

Print Materials
- Healing The Wounded Leader by Taquetta Baker
- Kingdom Keys To Governing Relationships by Taquetta Baker
- Sustaining The Visions Workbook by Taquetta Baker

Websites
- Olivetree.com
- Matthew Henry Strong's Online Concordance

Suggested reading:
- Kingdom Keys To Governing Relationships by Taquetta Baker
- Proverbs 31 The Marketplace Woman by Taquetta Baker
- Sustaining The Visions Workbook by Taquetta Baker
- Warlock Seduction by Jackie Green

Kingdom Shifters Product Line

Products available at kingdomshifters.com and amazon.com

Books (Paperback, Kindle, and e-books available)

Healing the Wounded Leader	There is an App for That
Apostolic Governing	Dance from Heaven to Earth
Apostolic Mantle	Annihilating Church Hurt
Healing the Wounded Leader	Discerning the Voice of God
Release the Vision	Feasting in His Presence
Birthing Books That Shift Generations	Prayers that Shift Atmospheres
Atmosphere Changes (Weaponry)	Dismantling Homosexuality
Strategies for Eradicating Racism	Let There Be Sight
Kingdom Shifters Decree That Thang	Kingdom Watchman Builder on the Wall
Kingdom Heirs Decree That Thang	Kingdom Keys to Governing Relationships
Fivefold Operations – Manuals I, II, and III	Unmasking the Power of the Scouts – Volumes I and II
Deliverance from the Suicide	Kingdom Wellness Counseling & Mentoring Manual I

Books for Liturgical / Interpretive Dance Ministries

Dance & Fivefold Ministry	Dance from Heaven to Earth
Spirits that Attack Dance Ministers	Dancers! Dancers! Dancers! Decree That Thang

CD's

Decree That Thang	Kingdom Heirs Decree That Thang
Teaching and Worship	